Praise for
TwentySomeone

"The decade of the twenties is one of major transition for most young adults. Unfortunately, many drift aimlessly through these critical years because they know neither the questions to ask nor the answers they need. Craig Dunham and Doug Serven have done a masterful job anticipating the questions young adults should be asking and helping them find the right answers. Every twentysomeone should profit from this book."

—JERRY BRIDGES, author of *The Pursuit of Holiness*
and staff member of The Navigators

"With personal transparency and spiritual insight Craig Dunham and Doug Serven offer wonderful insights that yield great opportunities for gospel transformation."

—BRYAN CHAPELL, president of Covenant Theological Seminary

"In *TwentySomeone*, Craig Dunham and Doug Serven generously share their journeys through their own twenties decade in a fresh, thoughtful, and practical style that builds a bridge between key questions in the young adult years and the experience of Christian faith. This book will serve as a 'mentor' for many."

—SHARON DALOZ PARKS, author of *Big Questions, Worthy Dreams: Mentoring Young Adults in Their Search for Meaning, Purpose, and Faith*

Twenty Someone

Twenty Someone

FINDING YOURSELF IN A DECADE OF TRANSITION

Craig Dunham & Doug Serven

WATERBROOK
PRESS

TWENTYSOMEONE
PUBLISHED BY WATERBROOK PRESS
2375 Telstar Drive, Suite 160
Colorado Springs, Colorado 80920
A division of Random House, Inc.

All Scripture quotations, unless otherwise indicated, are taken from the *Holy Bible, New International Version*®. NIV®. Copyright © 1973, 1978, 1984 by International Bible Society. Used by permission of Zondervan Publishing House. All rights reserved.

Many of the illustrations in this book reflect real names and stories and are used by permission. Names and details in a few stories have been changed to protect the identities of the persons involved.

ISBN 1-57856-695-9

Library of Congress Cataloging-in-Publication Data
Dunham, Craig.
    Twentysomeone : finding yourself in a decade of transition / Craig Dunham and Doug Serven.—1st ed.
        p. cm.
    Includes bibliographical references.
    ISBN 1-57856-695-9
    1. Church work with young adults. 2. Young adults—Religious life. I. Title: Twentysome-one II. Serven, Doug. III. Title
BV4446.D86 2003
248.8'4—dc22   2003016559

Printed in the United States of America
2004

10 9 8 7 6 5 4 3 2

For all the twentysomeones we have had the privilege of knowing,
learning with, and learning from.

Contents

Acknowledgments

I am beholden to my parents, Roger and Charlotte, as well as to my sisters, Jamie and Jill, for giving me all a boy could want growing up: a six-hundred-acre playground, freedom to explore it for hours on my own, and dinner together as a family when the day was done. This was the first environment I ever knew and the first in which I was encouraged to ask, "Who am I?" without fear of what the answers might be or require. Words cannot express my gratitude for this liberty.

I am also grateful to those who were the key influencers of my twenties: Larry Glabe, Jack and Shaunda McQueeney, Derek Strickler, and Brian Rutland. There have been many others who influenced me, but few did so as deeply and as faithfully as you did. I have been the better for it.

A word of gratitude is due The Navigators, who helped me to read, understand, and apply the Scriptures, and with whom I have now co-labored for ten years. I am honored to be among the ranks as just a small part of our enormous heritage and vision.

To all the staff who make up the Glen Eyrie Group, the camp and conference ministry of The Navigators, thank you for daily reminding me by your heart and example that the greatest among us is the one who serves. Our story has yet to be told…but will be one day.

I am grateful to everyone at WaterBrook Press, especially Elisa Stanford, whose enduring enthusiasm and developmental editing of this book were two reasons it ever got written. Thank you for taking a chance on us and for giving us this opportunity to publish our ideas.

Thank you to those writers—Ken Bradbury, Michael Card, Ken Gire, Adam Holz, Curry Kirkpatrick, Leura Jones, Dave McIntosh, Tim Mitchell, Scott Morton, Peg Ratliff, Dan Rich, Don Simpson, and Paul Stanley—for taking a genuine interest in my attempts (both past and present) at the craft. Your encouraging words have helped me persevere, and your talents of observation give me something to aspire to.

A special word of gratitude goes to all our donors and prayer supporters who have helped us in countless ways. Thank you for sticking with us and giving so generously.

Of course, to Doug, I can only say "grazie." You have somehow succeeded in keeping my idealism in check without negating the need for it in these pages. This book would not be what it is without your coauthorship, and I cannot think of anyone else with whom I would have rather written it. And to think that all this started with a "random" room assignment.

To my "skishies"—Maddie, Chloe, Katie, and Millie. You are each so amazingly your own little person, and I marvel at God's creativity in making you. One day I hope Daddy's ideas will make sense, help you, and cause you to laugh as you grow up and become even more of whom you have become so far.

I also want to thank Megan, my wife, who walked with me through a majority of my twenties and still didn't run from my answers to the question, Who am I? Your sense of commitment to what you believed in was what first attracted me to you, and now I am a beneficiary of that fierce and faithful devotion. I love you very much.

Thanks be to God…for everything.

—CRAIG DUNHAM

I am indebted to my mentors, some of whom I will have to wait to talk with in heaven—Augustine, Martin Luther, John Calvin, John Knox, Francis Schaeffer, C. S. Lewis. Others I may still get time (or more time) with in this life—Tim Keller, Brennan Manning, Os Guinness, Steve Garber, Bryan Chapell, Jack Collins, Hugh Barlett, Mark Davis, Chuck Garriott, Jerry Bridges, John Frame, and many others.

I'm grateful to The Navigators for teaching me the spiritual disciplines, to Covenant Seminary for showing me the Scriptures and the gospel, and to Reformed University Fellowship for calling me to be a pastor and for keeping me real. Not many people know of the ministry you do at RUF, but I do, and I think you're the greatest group of pastors I know. I'm humbled to be included in your number (mistakes do happen).

Some of you have invested heavily in my life, or you have imparted to me a love for learning more about God's creation: Dale Crutcher, Donna Turner, Denny Reeves, the MASUS gang, Larry Glabe, Mike Dodson, Jimmy Covey, the Heartland TLT, Dave Lovell, Don Guthrie, Esther Meek, the Covenant Seminary community, Chesterfield Presbyterian Church, Christ the King Church, Mike Biggs, and the North Texas Presbytery. Thanks for believing in me, but more important, for believing in the gospel in me.

Thanks to the RUF students and community at the University of Oklahoma—you've heard all this stuff a million times. Now you'll never escape it. Thanks for living out the gospel in front of me, teaching me more about Jesus, and allowing me to be your friend and pastor.

Thanks to all those who looked at this book along the way. There's no way I can mention all of you, but know that you have made it better by your gracious involvement, critique, and encouragement. You, Elisa, have believed in us all the way and have been essential in getting the book to where it is now.

Thanks to Craig. This book was your idea—thanks for including me in its vision and implementation. It's been a great ride these past fourteen years of knowing you. I pray this isn't the culmination of our friendship, just another step.

To my parents, Dan and Donna, and my sister and her husband, Denise and Dean—whoa. Can you believe it? Thanks for your love and support these thirty-plus years. Without you, I don't suppose I'd be here. Literally. You are "haminha"—the gift.

To my "tookies"—Ruth, Cal, Drew, and Anna. I love you and pray that you will love Jesus every day of your life, more and more, deeper and deeper. In one sense, this book is for you because I want you to be all God has intended you to be in your twenties and beyond. You make me laugh, make me crazy, make me call on God's grace, make me smile at your amazingness every day. I am so proud of you.

To my wife, Julie. You have stood by me for these past ten years as we've lived this book out. I love you. May the next ten be even better as we write *Thirty-Someone* in our lives together. Thanks for teaching me and loving me. You picture the gospel to me in so many ways. You're the most incredible person I know.

Soli Deo Gloria. My Redeemer lives.

—Doug Serven

Introduction

Those like myself whose imagination far exceeds their obedience are subject
to a just penalty; we easily imagine conditions far higher than any we have
really reached. If we describe what we have imagined we may make others,
and make ourselves, believe that we have really been there.

—C. S. LEWIS, *The Four Loves*

It's stasis that kills you off in the end, not ambition.

—BONO, *Rolling Stone* magazine

When I (Craig) was ten, Kurt Bielema and I thought it would be a swell idea to try our hand at aerial photography, detailing the many nuances of my family's one-hundred-year-old, six-hundred-acre farm in west central Illinois. Despite the fact that neither of us had our pilot's licenses (for obvious reasons—did I mention we were ten?), both of us were more creative than society should allow kids our age to be. This was not going to be a problem.

Rather than let mere inconvenience stop us, we rigged a heavy fifty-year-old Kodak something-o-matic camera I found in the attic to the underside of a cheap Batman kite. We then attached a separate line to the Kodak's plastic manual lever on the side. We had three rolls of kite string, each one thousand feet in length, and a howling wind blowing in from the north. Our plan was that once we got our survey gear in orbit—say about half a mile up—we'd pull the string attached to the camera and take a few shots. The scary thing was we were really serious about all this.

Unfortunately, after several tries and even more disappointment, we never got the kite-camera off the ground—the thing required more thrust and physics than we could provide. To add salt to our wounds, we had declared to our families that we were going to come back with satellite-quality photos from space; thus, we were in a bit of a bind.

To save face we went into a harvested cornfield, started jumping up and down with the camera pointed at the ground, and took a few pictures. It was a good try, but that's about all it was. In the end our families were not fooled by our attempt to present what we had not really captured.

In this book we want to provide a survey of the twenties—a real survey, no cornfield mock-ups—to help you discover yourself in the midst of this decade and make the most of your time there. Our ideas come from our own experiences and those of others, as well as some good old-fashioned observation, interpretation, and application of lessons. As we go along we'll do our best to ask and not assume, to prod and not preach, and to help instead of harass.

While we offer many practical suggestions at the end of most of the chapters, these aren't meant to be the meat of the book. Rather, they are suggestions and applications we and others have worked out with regard to the concepts we're talking about. Jumping quickly to those ends may work, but you will be like the blind squirrel that finds a nut once in a while—lucky.[1]

We'll warn you: We're new at writing about the twenties. But you're probably new at reading about them too. Maybe you're somewhere waiting for the subway or sipping cappuccinos in a bookstore or snuggled up with a blanket and some James Taylor playing in the background. We wrote this book for you because we think you are the ones who are really listening. You've tried some things, you've had the thought that it would be helpful to get a little guidance, and you're ready to pick up a book and consider what it says. Together we've been where you are (and recently too), and we think we can share a few thoughts to stimulate your thinking along your own quest.

This book aims at being real, which means we must deal with the ugliness of life in order to understand the glory of it as well. We hope to save you some grief by sharing with you a semiconcise approach to making sense of the process of discovering who you are and why it's important you know. We hope we'll help you feel a bit of weight come off your shoulders. And we hope to move you from being a twenty-some*thing* (and a cultural statistic) to being a

---

1. Providentially and sovereignly lucky, of course.

twenty-some*one* (and who God has made you to be), discovering and doing what you enjoy because you know what you enjoy and why.

Throughout the book we will offer some personal stories as well as concentrate on some enduring principles we've found helpful. Let us qualify this idea of principles, since anytime there are principles there are also exceptions. For instance, try completing this English example:

know/knew   grow/grew   throw/threw   _____/flew   snow/_____

In the first blank, *fly* doesn't follow the pattern established, but *flow/flew* just won't work. We tried, but in the second example, *snew*[2] doesn't quite fit either. The point? While we need patterns and principles, there are also ins and outs of life that have their own specific rules even when the principles are applied. While we always want to live by principles, we recognize the need to suspend them once in a while as well. Figuring all this out is how and when life gets interesting—and probably where you find yourself living right now.

We won't try to offer the ultradefinitive word on things, but we do want to provide insights we've gathered from our experiences over the past ten years. We hope they guide you through your own experiences and encourage you to interact with the book, yourself, and others as you examine your life thus far and consider what lies ahead.

One more thing: We've made a ton of mistakes and are in no way perfect people. In fact, we're two of the worst sinners we know who do too many stupid things to mention; but a book about all our sins doesn't sound like something you'd want to buy. We've tried to apply the principles we talk about, but by no means have things turned out roses all the time (that's the way it works—*snow/snew*, remember?). We've sought to learn from our mistakes, try anything once, and not get burned twice. So far it's been a good way to live.

As James Thurber once said, "You might as well fall flat on your face as

2. My (Doug's) daughter Ruth woke up one morning and said, "Mommy, it snew last night!"

lean over too far backwards."[3] Alas, we might. But let's at least fall forward together, dream some dreams, and figure out who we are in this decade of life so we can make a positive impact on those who will follow us.

In all of this, of course, we hope that it doesn't feel as if we're out in a cornfield jumping around with a camera. Here's hoping we get the kite in the air.

---

3. James Thurber, "The Bear Who Let It Alone," *New Yorker,* 29 April 1939.

CHAPTER ONE

The Question of
Our Twenties

*It will be in vain for me to stock my library, or organize societies,
or project schemes, if I neglect the culture of myself.*
—CHARLES HADDON SPURGEON, *Letters to My Students*

It doesn't happen all at once...you become. It takes a long time.
—MARGERY WILLIAMS, *The Velveteen Rabbit*

Mr. Craig Dunham is entering the decade of Career, Kids, and Marriage!"
So read the sign hanging on the door of my dorm room at the University of Missouri. These words, posted by the girl I was dating at the time, were also part of the first entry in my first-ever journal, dated February 5, 1991, the day I turned twenty.

While the sign seemed somewhat silly at the time, I think I missed its point. Career, kids, and marriage are all big things, sure, but they were just the tip of the iceberg of what was to come. You may not have had an embarrassing sign posted on your door on your twentieth birthday, but you might remember wondering what this new decade called "your twenties" would be like. And, like me, you may not have had a clue as to what you were getting yourself into.

Now when we say "your twenties," we don't mean to name a hard-and-fast delineation of time when we enter through one door and exit through another.[1] That would mean you have exactly ten years to figure everything out

---

1. But *Eighteen to Thirty-Five Someone* just didn't seem to work as a title.

and get going! We know that life does not necessarily respect age, nor does it give a rip as to how old or young we are when the proverbial poop begins to hit the fan. And since God made us different from one another, each of our experiences will be different.

But as different as *people* are, *life* is sometimes not quite as original. In other words, there are just some things (being on our own, figuring out what we believe, first job, first firing, career choices, car, house, getting married) that most of us encounter during our twenties. The reality is, most people experience more drastic life changes in their twenties than in any other stage of life, especially when we realize that marriage and kids and career—alone or in any combination—are going to be as much or more work than we thought they would be. With all these changes comes the need for good answers, and these good answers only come when we recognize our need for the right questions.

We trust that many of these issues are fresh in your mind. You're probably realizing that life isn't what you had expected in some areas and is far better than you had hoped it would be in others. How can we sort out these experiences and evaluate what we're all going through? Just what *is* the right question to ask?

The Most Important Question

What's the first question you were asked when you graduated from high school? We'll bet money it wasn't, "So, who are you going to become?" Are you kidding? It was, "So, what are you going to do now?" Although it's a fine question, performance immediately becomes the topic of conversation, reinforcing our behavior to please externally rather than be aware of our internal self. As a result of this mind-set, a lot of people in their twenties have no idea of their gifts and abilities, spiritual or otherwise. They might have a well-documented résumé but not be able to answer questions such as, "What are your strengths and weaknesses?"

While we may have an innate desire to know who we are, we may sense a lack of true identity in a world consumed with titles, positions, and stereotypes. We may start to believe the lie that, in the midst of a ridiculously paced culture, we just don't have time to stop and smell the roses. If it continues unchecked, this lack of time for reflection sets us up perfectly for the midlife crisis we've all heard about: We turn forty, change jobs, divorce our spouse, leave our kids, and run off with that cute guy or gal we met working out at Bally's, in hopes of "finding ourselves" by starting all over again. Or, for a scenario that is a bit milder, we may start to wonder if we've been in the wrong job all these years, our self-image may take some serious blows as we start to confront our mortality, and we might withdraw into a shell of television every night so we don't have to deal with any of these pounding thoughts.

Our twenties should not be as much about finding a job as about finding ourselves. Thus, the most important question to ask is not What do I do? but Who am I? This question can be difficult to answer because we may not know where to begin, but it is the key to understanding who God has made us and why—two important questions we need to answer in our twenties.

You may already be asking, "Who am I?" and perhaps you have attempted the "search for yourself" by way of experimentation—with drugs, sex, ideas, music, or rebellion. Whatever is different seems good in the quest for who you think you might be. In that scenario, however, who you are and who you are becoming comes not from within but from without.

The funny thing is, in answer to the question, Who am I? we're prescribing the same treatment: experiment. But not with drugs, sex, and rebellion. Rather, with concepts, jobs, groups, and places. The goal isn't to figure out the kind of person we *want* to be or the identity we think we *should* assume, but who it is God has *made* us to be and how *he* wants us to be identified. We need to experiment, to ask questions, and to explore to determine these things so that when we do commit ourselves to particular concepts, jobs, groups, and places, we'll have the assurance we're in the right place after all.

When we focus our energies on asking and answering the right questions, we begin to see what priorities we have or don't have. Of course, we could overdo all this and go on a ten-year vision quest, but that isn't quite what we're talking about here. In a nutshell, we're saying we should *take* the time to *make* the time to *evaluate* the time. We're talking about, for instance, valuing experiences over promotions, character over titles, and understanding over production.

For example, say you're presented with the opportunity to go to China for two years to teach English in an international school. Though you don't really want to teach for a living, you should consider how going to China could help you answer the who-am-I question. You may not end up going, but don't dismiss it out of hand. Consider the cultural difference it would make in your thinking if you walked on the Great Wall or came back with some deluxe chopsticks. Give some thought to the idea of returning to the United States and having great conversations with any one of the millions of Chinese people living here. Consider how such a trip would raise the bar in your evaluation of bad American Chinese restaurants.

Regardless of whether or not you go, you might find that if you can get out from under the pressure of the career track/corporate ladder to think for a moment about other options, you'll learn something about yourself. China may or may not be the best thing that could happen to you in the long run. The important thing is that you considered it as the possibility it could be. You thought through the decision in light of the who-am-I question.

How about character over titles? Which would you rather be: a sleazy corporate vice president or an honest busboy?[2] Is the desire to drive a Beemer really worth the sacrifice of character sometimes required to fulfill it? We all know the answer is no, but living out that answer (and being content with the probable outcome of doing so) is tough. A content heart and a humble spirit don't just happen. They take work, ultimately the work of Christ. At times character will cost us the titles, kudos, and perks we think we want.

Next, consider the balance between understanding and production. Many educational systems value the right answers in the right blanks. If we are raised primarily in that system, we might end up going through the motions to figure out what is on the "test" instead of learning the material and what it actually means. Sure, sometimes we just have to learn what's required, but that doesn't mean we have to stop there.

Other educational systems value exploration and creative problem solv-

---

2. Not that there aren't honest V.P.'s and sleazy busboys, mind you.

ing, relying more on what you *feel* than on what you *know.* This can keep us from the reality that truth is independent of our experiences and emotions. The point is to learn about the world in order to learn about ourselves and contribute a little something to civilization. This is a big deal, and now, not later, is the time to think about this stuff.

Why "Who Am I?"

From childhood we're raised with a presumed twelve to sixteen years of education as a standard prerequisite for "growing up."[3] As a result, we are accustomed to the idea that life is broken up into three- or four-year chunks (elementary, junior high, high school, college). We don't think twice about it; this is just how it is.

It comes then as a bit of a shock when we realize that the majority of our lives are not so segmented by "the system," and we are solely responsible for those years. Suddenly life seems short and our choices seem desperately critical. We start focusing on mere survival. Commitment to anything becomes scary because we think we have so much to lose.

As we pursue work, career, and family, we need to relax and give ourselves permission to try different things and experience life for the first time on our own, not wallowing in desperation about those monumental decisions that "have" to be made. The reality is that where we go to college usually doesn't come back to haunt us or "get us in" somewhere. We may make decisions based on what career path we think we want to travel or which ladder of success we think we want to climb, but the truth is, most people end up with a job that has only a slim connection with their college major.[4] We may think something will be exciting, but instead it turns out to be excruciating. We dread the idea of taking one opportunity, and lo and behold,

---

3. We realize that this hasn't always been the case. If you were born in a different time or place you'd have been "grown up" long ago. Adolescence is a fairly new idea. But here we are, so we have to deal with our place in life here and now.
4. Us, for example.

something absolutely life changing ends up happening. Life and our enjoyment of it are simply not determined by the first decision we make, whether good or bad.

In their book *Repacking Your Bags*, Richard Leider and David Shapiro write:

> Life is not meant to be linear. The path from birth to death is not a straight-line journey; it's a zig-zag.... The linear point of view says first get an education, then work hard, then retire so you can finally begin living. But by that time, many people have forgotten how to live, or else they're so exhausted by getting to where they've gotten that there's no life left. The alternative is to live all your life as fully as possible. To challenge the existing script. To wander as opposed to sticking to the straight and narrow. Of course, this is scary and isn't easy, as it means we have to continually ask questions about our life, our love, our work.[5]

Let's face it: If the average life span of a person is, say, seventy years, one or two years are not going to have that much of a detrimental impact on the overall outcome of our lives. Even if we forgo that internship we were offered, graduate late, take a year off to work, or do whatever else we've thought about doing, success and accomplishment are just not that dependent on our making every decision perfectly or within a self-induced time frame. Our view of God needs to be bigger than that.

We sometimes forget that some of the greatest people in history didn't make their marks on the world until they hit their thirties, forties, fifties, or even sixties. Instead, we allow our culture to pressure us into having everything figured out and wrapped up in a nice, neat little package by the time we're twenty-five years old. Is this realistic? Is this healthy? Is this how it usually works? We don't think so.

---

5. Richard Leider and David Shapiro, *Repacking Your Bags* (San Francisco: Berrett-Koehler, 1996), 76-7.

The Chance of a Lifetime

We can't adequately consider the answer to the question, Who am I? without the intention, encouragement, or structure with which to process it. And yet, as you've probably already experienced, in the workplace, the classroom, and even the church, personal *development* is not valued as much as personal *production*. This should not be, but unfortunately we don't see things changing anytime soon—unless the change begins with us.

It can be a frightening proposition. In J. R. R. Tolkien's *The Two Towers*, the hobbits are lost in the forest, and Aragorn is trying to figure out if his small troop should undertake the dangerous task of going after them. Finally, after some consideration, he says to his friends, "There are some things that are better to begin than to refuse, even though the end may be dark."[6] So it is with us.

None of us knows what lies ahead. We'll probably experience amazing times of rapturous joy as we live life to the fullest as well as times of anguish when we wonder if we can exit the bed once more in the morning. In a sense, we don't have a choice to stop completely and get our lives together because life happens regardless, but in another way we can take Aragorn's challenge and begin the journey of finding ourselves along the way. We can go for it with all we have, knowing that the journey will most certainly entail battles and rests, goblins and companions, and maybe even some mystical elven wine and dancing at Rivendell when all is said and done.

Regardless of the details, this is your big chance to make the most of your twenties. Sure, you're busy, and yes, you have other things to do. And you're human and make mistakes. But now is your chance—the chance of a lifetime!—to make the most of the rest of this amazing decade by taking the time

---

6. J. R. R. Tolkien, *The Two Towers* (New York: Ballantine, 1963), 53. The parallel we're trying to draw here is inspiring, except for the "dark" thing. Not sure what to tell you on that one, except that while Aragorn and the crew end up in a bunch of caves with little to eat before eventually finding the hobbits and saving the day, maybe the worst that will happen to you is that you'll end up in a poorly lit coffee shop sipping bad coffee. Who knows?

to do things thoughtfully and prayerfully, answering the question, Who am I? as you go.

Our prayer for you is that you come to embrace the idea that the decade of the twenties is the most strategic decade of development in your life.[7] In the midst of a barrage of new experiences and opportunities, your patterns of thinking develop and change. The foundations of your character and world-view begin to solidify, and upon them you will eventually build the structures of your life. How you manage and evaluate this decade of time has a direct impact on the integration of your theology, person, and aspirations for years to come.

The journey starts in earnest now, for as the map in the mall reads, "You are here."

---

7. There, we said it.

CHAPTER TWO

God Has a Wonderful
(and Strange and Confusing)
Plan for Your Life

[Approaching God] is not a matter of miles but of experience.
—A. W. TOZER, *The Pursuit of God*

He became what we are that He might make us what He is.
—IRENAEUS

One morning over a recent Thanksgiving holiday, I (Doug) was in my old college town of Columbia (where Craig and I met), walking around the University of Missouri campus. I remembered my first weekend at college: After an emotional drop-off by my parents, my first roommate, Coy Stine, and I walked around campus in awe of our newfound freedom. *We can do anything we want right now, and no one would ever know,* we thought. I couldn't believe the sense of opportunity that lay before us.

Growing up in small-town Missouri, I, like everyone else, yearned for attention. I had achieved some level of popularity in high school through semiachievement in sports and a sarcastic wit, the latter of which I look back on now with some regret. A certain sense of invincibility grew inside me until I believed I could get my way at any time or in any venture.

Thankfully, God didn't leave me alone. He worked to humble me, and the fifteen years that have passed since those first weeks of college have been full. A "sea of opportunity" was out there for me to discover (insert your own high-school graduation speech here), and sometimes I went for it. At other times I retracted into a shell, walling myself off. The great times were interspersed with some awful, despondent times—chipping away at arrogance is a slow and painful process. Somehow those experiences came together, though, and in the process I figured out that these highs, lows, and plateaus, and how we deal with them are what life is all about.

The Detours of a Developer God

Most people in their twenties have a bit (or a bunch) of anxiety about the upcoming events of the next five years, months, weeks, or even days. You may be in your midtwenties and already into a career, but the future may still look a little murky. While there are those few who have decided the direction of their futures, they tend to be the exceptions and not the rule.[1] The same ratio applies to the collection of characters in the Bible. God has given us plenty of examples of people who didn't have everything figured out. Rest assured, if you don't know what you're going to do with your life, you're in good company.

The good thing is that although God uses people who are mostly clueless, he in fact is not. He is aware of everything that happens throughout history and directs everything with a knowing and watchful eye—a fact that can intimidate us when we're young believers. This is not necessarily bad; such an idea should boggle our minds and breed in us a spirit of respect and gratitude for God's hand in our lives.

At some point, though, a transition can take place, moving us from a once-healthy respect of God's omniscience and sovereignty to a relaxed and lazy view of his power. Sure, God's sovereignty is astounding and real because it brought us to salvation.[2] But when it comes to what we do with our lives— who we marry, if we marry, how many kids we have, where we live, if we go to Africa, etc.—well, we're not so sure God knows what he's doing anymore. We forget who started all this and figure it's up to us to finish it.

---

1. They also tend to be engineers.
2. See Ephesians 1.

The truth is, God tends to take us from point A to point Z *through* points B, C, D, E, and so on. In other words, we don't just arrive somewhere; we go through a process along the way. God uses the intermediate experiences to mold us into what he wants us to be. Often this period of uncertainty—the times when we can't see how something fits into the broader plan of God—is training for our trusting him. It also helps us discover ourselves along the way. Our faith in God is to become a way of life, not a one-time event, and our faithfulness in following him—no matter the circumstance or our degree of understanding—is crucial to being at peace in our twenties.

All this can be overwhelming. But we believe God will always lead us in a way in which we will eventually recognize his doing so. And yet you probably noticed we said *eventually*. Our reasoning goes like this: God is as much concerned with our development as he is with our direction. He works to satisfy this dual purpose for each of us, and this can feel like a million detours in our lives.

Acts 27 gives us a good example of keeping perspective in the midst of detour. The apostle Paul was traveling as a prisoner to Rome—what we think was his final destination here on earth. After making slow headway for many days, the ship he was on was sailing along the shore of Crete when Paul predicted a disastrous voyage if they continued. Ignoring his advice and taking that of the pilot and the owner of the ship, a majority of the crew decided to keep sailing. Before long, a northeaster swept down from the island and, true to Paul's prediction, by the third day of hurricane-force winds, most people on the ship had given up all hope of ever being saved.

As the story goes, Paul gave a bit of an "I told you so," but then encouraged the crew to keep up their courage because God had shown him that not one of them would be lost if they stayed with the ship. He then broke the news that they would run aground soon. (Paul always did know how to silence a crowd.) Sure enough, they shipwrecked.

Forgetting Paul's words, the men began doing what seemed logical: They lowered the lifeboats to bail out. But Paul reminded them of what God had told him about staying with the ship. Considering Paul's track record up to this point, the men finally made the right application: They cut the ropes that held the lifeboats and let them fall away.

Before dawn the next morning, Paul encouraged the crew to eat all they could before throwing the rest of the grain overboard. Again, this probably didn't make much sense to seasoned sailors shipwrecked in the middle of the sea, but they did it anyway. As the sun came up, they saw the sandy beach of an island and decided to swim for it. The Scriptures record that "in this way everyone reached land in safety" (Acts 27:44). The island was inhabited, and the people showed kindness to the crew. Roughly three months later, they made it to Rome.

Was God toying with Paul and the crew? Was he being cruel in allowing or causing (depending on your theology) their shipwreck to happen? We could argue as much, except for the fact that throughout the experience God spoke to Paul about it, explaining to him his means of salvation (staying with the ship) and comforting him while Paul and the crew waited to be saved. Francis Schaeffer describes the importance of understanding God to be not just "God" but rather "the God Who is there."[3] God used the shipwrecked cruise to Rome to build in Paul and the crew a deeper understanding of that ever-present God.

Just as God spoke to Paul in the midst of his detour, the God Who Is There speaks to us in the midst of ours. In the above passage we can see three truths about those who are "in Christ":

1. God loves us and will not forget us because he has engraved us on the palms of his hands (see Isaiah 49:15-16).
2. God has a plan to prosper us and not to harm us (see Jeremiah 29:11).
3. God will finish the work he has begun in and through us (see Philippians 1:6).

As hurricane-force winds toss us in life, the question is not *if* God has spoken. The question is, Have we listened and cut the ropes of our lifeboats instead of bailing out?

---

3. For a unique metaphysical discussion on the question of whether God is or isn't "the God Who is there," read Schaeffer's *He Is There and He Is Not Silent* (Wheaton, Ill.: Tyndale, 2001). Whoa.

Thinking About God

Many people think the word *theology* is bad, a concept that brings about bickering and division. But theology is simply this: thoughts about God. We all have them, even if they lurk only in our subconscious and rise up just once in a while. We even have a theology if we practically reject God, because doing so admits the concept of him.

We should begin in our twenties (or earlier) to cultivate a life of reflection about who God is—a life of theology. Even if you say, "I just want to love Jesus," you've entered into theology: Which Jesus are you talking about? Throughout the centuries people have had many ideas about who Christ is, and surely you haven't figured it out completely, have you? "Just loving Jesus" is far more complicated than saying you do; it takes a lifetime to wrap our minds around the meaning of this so-called simple thing.[4] Making sure our concept of God is right and biblical is our first priority, but working on that theology is a lifetime project.

Thinking about God helps us understand him more, and this is essential to making sense of the world around us. John Calvin wrote, "Nearly all the wisdom we possess, that is to say, true and sound wisdom, consists of two parts: the knowledge of God and of ourselves." This two-part approach—knowing God in order to know more of who he made us to be—is precisely what we're talking about. Calvin continues:

> But, while joined by many bonds, which one precedes and brings forth
> the other is not easy to discern. In the first place, no one can look
> upon himself without immediately turning his thoughts to the con-
> templation of God.... The knowledge of ourselves not only arouses us
> to seek God, but also, as it were, leads us by the hand to find Him.[5]

---

4. Jonathan Edwards said, "Men often do not see or allow the consequences of their own doctrines." Ouch. (Jonathan Edwards, *The Works of Jonathan Edwards,* vol. 1 [Peabody, Mass.: Hendrickson, 2000], 529.)
5. John Calvin, *Institutes,* bk. 2, ed. John T. McNeill, trans. Ford Lewis Battles (1536; reprint, Louisville, Ky.: Westminster John Knox, 1960), 35.

Knowing God and knowing ourselves are intertwined; starting with one will lead to the other.

When we first consider God and what he is like, we can begin with ideas like "loving," "kind," "good," "sovereign," "in control," "Master," "Jesus," "Holy Spirit," and "Father." These are good words and reveal our concept of the One who made everything and holds it all in his hands. The Westminster Shorter Catechism[6] says that God is a spirit, infinite, eternal, unchangeable in his being, wisdom, power, holiness, and truth. This is another great list.

If we are deep-down honest, though, we may also have some negative images mulling around in our thoughts of who God is—controlling, manipulative, or mean. For example, the idea of God as Father may bring up feelings of abuse, disappointment, or abandonment if your own dad didn't love you as he should have. While our experiences of God do not define him, they do influence our perceptions of him, so it's important to recognize and explore the ways we think of God.

God is wholly *other* than us. This is sometimes called his "transcendence." He is a spirit, infinite and unchangeable in his being. He created everything. He judges us and understands and controls how the whole world is working, down to the caterpillar's next meal. Because of God's omnipotence, we can sometimes forget that he is also good—always good—even if we don't understand at times how that can be.

We must remember that God is also perfectly relational, and he initiates relationship with his people. This is called his "immanence"—he has come to us in a covenantal relationship. This relationship is depicted in many ways—we are ransomed from slavery, saved from death, married even though we were unfaithful, judged by a Holy One, and brought near as one estranged—but the overwhelming picture we get of God throughout the Bible is *Father*, One who cares for and lovingly disciplines his children. Over and over again we get the idea that we are adopted.

Jack Miller, the founder of World Harvest Mission, wrote about the dif-

---

6. An amazing seventeenth-century document that discusses who God is and how he works in the world.

ference between living as orphans and living as sons and daughters. An orphan lives an unknown, insecure, and abandoned life. Orphaned children try to prove their worth to others so they might be thought "good" enough to be adopted. In contrast, adopted sons and daughters live in the freedom of the care of loving parents and family. They experience the blessings of new status and can grow and learn and live life to the fullest because they know they are loved and accepted. What a difference!

As parents, my wife, Julie, and I (Doug) tell our kids we love them no matter what, but we still expect them to pick up their rooms, put on their jammies, and do the things that are part of being in our household. They aren't doing those things to prove that they love us or to secure their places within our family, but rather (we hope) out of a sense of love. This motivation may not always be there, but our goal as parents is to encourage them to see participation in our family as a whole-life experience born out of love rather than obligation. Likewise, in our faith the greater goal is to be motivated by love, not by a fear of displeasing God. The more we understand God's love, the more motivated we are to obey him.

Think about your heart. Is yours the heart of an orphan or that of a cherished son or daughter? Or are you an already-adopted son or daughter who is still living like an orphan?

Rich Mullins once said in a concert: "God notices you. The fact is he can't take his eyes off of you. However badly you think of yourself, God is crazy about you. God is in love with you. Some of us even fear that someday we'll do something so bad that he won't notice [us] anymore. Well, let me tell you, God loves you completely. And he knew us at our worst before he ever began to love us at all. And in the love of God there are no degrees, there is only love."[7]

With this idea of adopted "sonship" and "daughtership" in mind, we can begin to understand more fully how God didn't just generally make *all* of us; he specifically made *each* of us. As Psalm 139 tells us, even before we were born, God knew us. This knowing isn't a vague awareness, it is a special care

---

7. Rich Mullins, remarks at a concert in Anderson, Indiana, 16 November 1995.

and a warm devotion that comes from and leads to relationship. God became like one of us in order to bring us into his family. He didn't have to, but because of his grace, he adopted us. This truth should bring us to our knees. The God Who Is There knew us—and still does. How then can we live the life our Father desires for us?

Responding to Our Callings

So this adoptive father God cares about who we are and who we are becoming. He also cares about what we do. He has made each of us for a particular purpose, not just for our sakes but for the sake of others. In his wonderful book *Let Your Life Speak,* Parker Palmer writes, "True vocation joins self and service, as Frederick Buechner asserts when he defines vocation as 'the place where your deep gladness meets the world's deep need.' "[8] Wherever you are in your twenties, it might be good to reevaluate your decisions in light of your primary and secondary callings.

Our Primary Calling

Our primary calling comes out of our true identity as redeemed children of God, children of his creation. At the beginning of time, God made everything, and he made it all very good. Genesis 1–2 give us the description of this work, emphasizing the One who created out of love. God formed Adam and Eve as a special creation who would bear in them the *imago dei,* the image of God. Nothing else, no other creature, has the *imago dei,* and this makes us amazingly special, set apart from the rest of creation as a masterpiece.

Adam and Eve, then, as special creations bearing the image of God, resided with God in the Garden of Eden in perfect fellowship and community with him. Have you ever imagined what that would have been like? Picture it for a moment. Think of what it would have been like to talk to God and immediately hear him. To know him—right there!

Got it? Now let's move to Genesis 3 and feel the weight of the Fall. We

---

8. Parker Palmer, *Let Your Life Speak* (San Francisco: Jossey-Bass, 2000), 16.

had it all and gave it up for a lie; Satan duped us, and we traded glory for nothing. Argh! From that point on, God has been reclaiming and redeeming his people in an eternal love story. As we trace the redemption of God's people to himself throughout the Scriptures, we can see the unfolding of the story and who we are in it. This is *our* story; these are *our* people. We are not only in this sinful condition because of what Adam did—*we* did it as well. We are sinful people, people who keep doing wrong and don't always do the things we should.[9] We have no right to the love of God. We deserve his condemnation because we have treated him as an enemy, spitting in his face despite his good gifts to us. Francis Schaeffer calls us "glorious ruins," for each of us has the *imago dei* in us, but we have been shattered and broken by sin. Jeremiah 17:9 says that our hearts are deceitful above all things, and Isaiah 64:6 says that even our righteous acts are like filthy rags[10] to God.

But…"because of his great love for us, God, who is rich in mercy, made us alive with Christ even when we were dead[11] in transgressions—it is by grace [we] have been saved" (Ephesians 2:4-5). What is grace? Grace is "undeserved favor for those who deserve God's wrath."[12] How awesome is that? God loves us even when we don't deserve it, even when we actually deserve the exact opposite. He adopts us, calls us, redeems us, changes us, cares for us, gifts us, and sets us apart because of what he did for us. We not only become God's sons and daughters, but Jesus Christ becomes our brother—and God, amazingly enough, loves us "even as" or "just as" he loves Christ! Check that out in Jesus' prayer in John 17:23, and stand with your jaw dropped as you realize how much God loves you—as much as he loves Jesus himself. This is exciting

---

9. The Westminster Confession defines sin as "any want of conformity to the law of God or transgression of the law of God." That means it's not only doing the wrong things we're not supposed to do, but it's also not doing the right things we are supposed to do. A double whammy.

10. Literally like what a woman would use to absorb the flow of blood during her period.

11. The Greek word for *dead* here means "dead." We are not "slightly out of it" or "just a bit groggy" in our sins; we are dead in them. To clarify, dead people can do nothing for themselves but rot and smell.

12. Jerry Bridges helped us with this definition through his books (such as *The Discipline of Grace*) and a few personal conversations.

stuff! God calls us to repent and become his children. This is good news. This is the gospel.

The apostle Paul talks about all of this grace and adoption with "in him" language: We are clothed "in Christ"; "he chose us in him"; "in him we have redemption"; "you were included in Christ." These phrases are all over the place, particularly in Ephesians 1. What does all this "in-him-ness" mean? It means that we are no longer completely our own, and Jesus has become the Lord of our lives in every area imaginable. He makes us who we were made to be in the first place: free and ready to live life to the fullest.[13]

So our primary calling is to live out our identity as children of God, children who have been restored by the pursuing, loving, merciful God to the relationship with him we were intended to have all along.[14] Truly understanding and embracing this relationship and growing in it deeper every day transforms us in our dealings with the world. When we see our primary calling as being a beloved son or daughter of God, we can reject other callings to make career or kids or beauty or promotions our foundation. We can be content with what we have and don't have, stopping our ears to the siren calls of the world and taking joy and peace in our standing with Christ.

Our Secondary Calling

Our secondary calling is a little different. It means living the particular peculiarity of being a beloved child of God in all the ways he has made you. If you are a Christian, you may notice something: You are still you. God may have changed some passions in your life, and you no longer have certain desires or cravings that you may once have had. That's good; you need to look different from the world in the way you approach life. But did your appearance change? Did you suddenly get a smaller nose or different color hair? No, and although

---

13. See John 10:10.

14. If this relationship isn't clear to you or you recognize that you do not have it, ask the Savior of the world to invade your life and make you whole again. He promises he will be near to those who seek him. Admit your need for cleansing, come clean with the wrong you have done, and ask for forgiveness from the One who died on the cross for your sins and lived the perfect life on your behalf.

your personality might change a bit as a result of your inner sense of peace and growth in the fruit of the Spirit, fundamentally you are still the same person. This consistency shows the *imago dei* in every person, believer and nonbeliever, because God has created each of us to be a unique reflection of his image. This "us-ness" is special and begins the unfolding of our secondary calling.

In our twenties, our calling often seems to fluctuate with our circumstances, never mind our convictions. We want so badly to know what we are to do and why, yet most people don't get a true sense of their secondary calling until they get into their forties! This may not seem like good news, but it presents an interesting notion to consider: Could it be that God holds off the full revealing and fulfillment of that secondary calling until later in life so that earlier in life we can focus on other things, namely who we are and who we are becoming?

It's true that God is perpetually at work, awakening in us desires, creating an initial interest or two that may later turn into a full-blown passion, but always directing us along the sovereign path he has planned for us since the beginning of time.[15] But in our experience, secondary callings come later and not sooner. That's okay because it gives us time to evaluate that calling in light of the right question: Who am I?

Considering Our SHAPE

So how do we begin the process of discovering our secondary calling? One way we've found helpful is to consider our lives in light of our SHAPE: our spiritual gifts, heart, abilities, personality, and experiences.[16]

Spiritual Gifts

The teaching and discerning of spiritual gifts is often neglected in our churches today. As a result, in our twenties most of us haven't stopped to consider this

---

15. Again, look at Ephesians 1, especially verse 11.
16. The SHAPE acronym is from CLASS 301, published by Pastors.com. Copyright 1988 by Rick Warren. Used with permission of Pastors.com, Inc. All rights reserved.

important part of our spiritual makeup and how it factors into our contributions to the church and to the culture.

Take a quick stroll through 1 Corinthians 12 and Romans 12 to familiarize yourself with the kinds of gifts you're trying to identify in your life. When we become Christians, the Holy Spirit gives each of us gifts to build up the body of Christ and make it function the way God intended. Paul described this using the analogy of a whole body made up of many different parts. Each of us has been given different gifts that, when all are put together, allow us to function as the church is intended to, in wholeness. As we use these gifts, we glorify God and help other people in a way that is both natural—because we enjoy it and it looks like everyday stuff—and supernatural—because it is powered by the Holy Spirit in us and not necessarily by our own initiative.

While there are plenty of good tests and resources to help you begin to figure out how God has gifted you, start by thinking about two things: (1) What are some of the gifts in 1 Corinthians and Romans that you get fired up about? What do you gravitate toward doing? Which gifts do you look for ways of using in the world and your church? and (2) Which of these gifts have you seen bear fruit in your life? In other words, what areas of your life have others confirmed? What gifts have others seen in you and affirmed? You may want to ask others to give you feedback on the gifts they see in your life. As the answers come together, and as you begin to test them in your life and ministry, you will begin to discern what gifts the Holy Spirit has given you.

We should note a few other things as well. First, as you consider the list again, you may find yourself desiring certain gifts that you want to have or think you should have. That's because our culture and churches sometimes "rank" the gifts in a specific order of importance based on visibility and status. Don't fall into that trap! Seek what the Lord has given you and learn how to make the most of it, regardless of what your gift is or how many or few gifts you have.

Second, reading this list and thinking about your gifts doesn't mean you'll get it nailed down right at first. You may need more time to try different things and gain new experiences—we suggest this, in fact—to see what it is you like and don't like to do. Some gifts may be quite obvious while others are tucked away; you might not discover and cultivate those until later. That's okay; just be intentional in taking time to uncover what your gifts are as best you can.

Finally, while not all the gifts will be in your area of natural or supernatural passion, you still need to exercise them. For instance, just because you don't have the spiritual gift of mercy doesn't mean you can excuse yourself from helping people in need. In a sense, it's like what you experienced if you went to college—you pick a major and take more elective classes in that area, but at the same time you have general requirements because other areas of life and study are also important. Pursue your passions, but don't neglect the other "prerequisites" in doing so.

Heart

The light in the bathroom of my (Doug's) local coffee shop goes on by a motion sensor. For some reason I get a bit of a thrill when I open the door and it's dark in there just before the light goes on and reveals that no one has used the bathroom for a while.[17]

In the same way my presence and movement trigger the light in the bathroom, so God trips the light in our hearts when we start to explore ourselves a bit. We may enter areas that haven't been visited in a while; they might be dark and drafty or possibly a little cold and dirty. But as we move and explore with the light of God's Spirit illuminating the caverns of our souls, we may feel more at home, maybe even deciding to stay a bit longer and find out what's really in there.

To start understanding more of what's going on in your heart, ask yourself, What is it I'm passionate about? People, painting, travel, learning, jazz, scrapbooks, snipe hunting, eating at Eskimo Joe's? Our heart's passions reveal our desires. They're a big part of what make us who we are. If we don't pursue the passions contained within our desires (the good ones, that is) because they're impractical or we think they're silly or we're too busy, we run the risk of losing a major part of ourselves. So once you figure out what you're passionate about, cultivate those things. We need to care for our hearts and

17. Okay, so that's weird.

passions—examine them, write about them, share them, express them—or we will grow cold and disconnected as we pursue things in life we don't really care about.

Our heart's passions can break through the busyness of life and the lack of worth our society may place on such things. Think about the practical value of art, for instance. It's really just colors on canvas or shapes carved out of stone. Nothing more. And yet art can stir us in ways that are difficult to express with words. We need to take the time to discover and do the things that bring us life. We can't completely ignore the practical side of life, but we need to carve out time—either daily, weekly, or monthly—to do the things that pump energy into us and make us the people we are.

Eventually, we'll find ourselves doing the things that ignite our passion without even realizing it. When we (Doug and Julie) were trying to get our son Cal to keep his undies dry at night, it was a celebration when he did it and sadness when he didn't. Every once in a while, we'd be awakened by the faint rustling of movement and then an eventual flush and scampering back to bed. Cal had made it to and from the bathroom by himself, on his own initiative! After one successful night I talked to Cal about his accomplishment, raining down praise on him. He wasn't sure what I was talking about since he'd only been about half-awake when it happened. I assured him that he'd kept his undies dry by getting up and going to the bathroom by himself. "Dad," he said, "I didn't even see myself!" We, too, will be saying, "I didn't even see myself" when we are living in line with our heart's passions.

Abilities

As we think more about who we are with our hearts unwrapped a bit, we should take time to discern our abilities. Spiritual gifts and talents can overlap (for example, the gift of administration and the ability that accompanies being a math whiz), but they can also be quite different from one another. There are only a handful of gifts and literally hundreds of abilities.

To start off, take notes on what you like to do. Usually what we like to do is what we're best at. Isn't it just like God to correlate the two—to not only help us identify our abilities but also to provide us with some enjoyment in the midst of them?

What skills do you have? What are the things you are really, really good at and enjoy doing? What have others thanked you for doing that they could not? These may seem like simple questions, but we're always surprised at how few people in their twenties can knock off a list of their talents and abilities.[18]

One way to identify our abilities is to recognize what they are not. For instance, I (Craig) am not exactly the handiest person in the world—about the only thing I can do with a tool is lose it. Even though I grew up as a farm kid with a dad who had a thirty-foot-long workbench, a stash of quality tools, and all the odds and ends you could ever dream of in a barn, the idea of going beyond my LEGOs (and later my Erector Set) never crossed my mind; I just wasn't wired that way. Because construction didn't exactly "raise my roof," I didn't feel the need to pursue it. Instead, I gave myself to things like sports, music, writing, graphic design—things I was much better at and enjoyed much more.

Another way to determine what our skills are is to get honest feedback from others who have a clue. Let us stress that last part—*who have a clue*—as being the key phrase here. Your grandpa is always going to say you have a lovely singing voice, but what you may not know is that grandpa has been tone-deaf since birth. Your friends may think your comedy routine is as funny as their favorite sitcom, but that may or may not be the highest compliment they can pay you. (Though if it is, well, congratulations.)

When we set out to write this book, we got a lot of positive feedback from people—friends, families, twentysomethings—who read parts of it. Everyone seemed to like our ideas and how we wrote about them. Everyone, that is, except for the people who could and would actually fork over the dough to publish it. While we passionately believed in what we were doing, our publisher

---

18. One time, my (Craig's) wife, Megan, was doing a staff interview for Eagle Lake, The Navigators' summer camp for kids. When she asked, "What skills do you have?" the response from the twenty-one-year-old interviewee was, "Well, I don't cuss." Hmmmm.

friends were the ones who helped us hone and polish our writing because they had the perspective and experience to be able to do so. It took honest, not just positive, feedback from people who had a clue to further develop and affirm any abilities we might have had in what we were trying to do.

However we choose to go about discovering our abilities, the point is to go about doing it. We should try new things, remember what we learn as we succeed or fail at them, and make future decisions based on this increasing body of information as we seek to answer the who-am-I question.

Personality

Our individual personalities set us apart from the rest of God's creation because they translate to expressions of art and emotion, two elements that do not exist outside the human world.[19] Along with our spiritual gifts, heart, and abilities, our personality is an important component of learning more of what makes us who we are.

The two of us provide a good example of different personalities. Doug is more laid back and go-with-the-flow, never really late but never really early either. I (Craig) am more structured and compulsive, fifteen minutes ahead of schedule for most things. Doug is more extroverted; I'm more introverted.[20] At Mizzou, Doug was better at leading our campus Navigators meetings, cutting up with comedy and yet still connecting well with the students. I was better at making sure we knew what we were talking about the next week, planning and coordinating details months in advance.

It's not that Doug doesn't enjoy time alone, or that I'm *always* alone. We are just two different people. While we could most likely *survive* in each other's

---

19. In *Life After God* (New York: Pocket Books, 1995), Douglas Coupland has identified three other expressions that do not exist outside the human world: smoking, body-building, and writing.

20. A funny story: One long weekend during our junior year of college, we were invited to go to Washington, D.C., for the Presidential Prayer Breakfast. Doug was the life of his group, and they saw every sight in town. I (Craig) stayed in my hotel room and slept, exhausted from the extroversion of it all. Doug was so mad at me, he asked at least three times on the flight back to Columbia, "How do you go to Washington, D.C., and spend the entire weekend in a hotel room?" There was no good answer.

environments, we probably wouldn't *thrive*. Just as the structure of an eight-to-five daily schedule would easily take the life from Doug,[21] without a doubt, the *lack* of structure in Doug's job would be the absolute end of me. We've learned this by collecting and comparing notes, and this has been an invaluable part of answering, Who am I?

So how do you begin to characterize your personality? Thousands of years ago the ancient Greeks asked the same question. They developed a system of temperaments based on their theories of human physiology, or "humors," as first proposed by Empedocles.[22] While these particular connections are largely dismissed today, they were an integral part of Greek beliefs then. Their four distinct temperament categories (now known as choleric, phlegmatic, sanguine, and melancholic) have been used in recent years as part of various personality tests.

Tests don't determine our personalities, but they can help reveal characteristics of our personalities. Do you derive more energy from being alone or from being with people? Do you figure out problems by collecting data with your senses, or do you usually make an intuitive educated guess to get an answer? When you come across a situation, do you like to think about it for a while and mull it over in your mind, or do you react with feeling first? Do you like to make lists, be organized, and get through tasks, or would you rather go with the flow, see what happens, and keep your options open? Congratulations, you just took a very scaled-down version of the Myers-Briggs Type Indicator (MBTI).

What about other characteristics? Are you aggressive, domineering,

---

21. Another sort-of-funny story: Not that long ago Doug actually did try to do something similar to my job. (He obviously needed to read this book.) With an eight-to-five schedule, Excel spreadsheets, business meetings, long-range planning, memos, and PowerPoint presentations, he came home seriously depressed and miserable every day because he was working completely outside his calling and gifting. That led him to where he is now.

22. Humoral theory states that there are four body fluids (blood, phlegm, yellow bile, and black bile), and their proper mixture is the condition of health. Astrologers later began associating the various temperaments with the elements (earth, fire, water, and air) and the symbols of the Zodiac.

passive, a dreamer, a visionary, a go-getter, a server, a mothering person, woodsy, practical, sarcastic, quick-witted, gregarious? Make a list of what you'd say as well as what you think others would say about you. If you get really brave, ask others for their own list on you. You could also read *Winnie the Pooh* and determine which of A. A. Milne's characters running around the Hundred Acre Wood you most identify with.[23] Or ask some of your close friends what they think your strengths and weaknesses are. Whatever route you take in evaluating yourself, figuring out your personality tendencies will help you see where you can best contribute in most situations as well as help you feel more at home with yourself and your temperament.

Just keep one thing in mind: Jesus is the only one who had a perfect personality, which we believe was an amazing combination of all of them. He never fell into the sinful tendencies each personality type can bring out. He could (and did) act perfectly and appropriately in each and every situation. Since we aren't quite in that place ourselves, we must know where our personalities best shine and also where they need even more redeeming. Understanding our natural tendencies doesn't give us license to act because "that's just the way I am," but it does help us realize how much we need Christ in our lives to mold and shape us to be more like him.

Experiences

In a world quickly losing its grasp on all things original, our experiences (no matter how goofy or strange they may seem) are part of us and make us who we are. They teach us the thrill of the search and the fun of discovery. Like our fingerprints, none of us has the same set of experiences. Sure, our experiences may be similar, but they will never be an exact match with someone else's. Our experiences provide a great way to answer the question, Who am I? as we capitalize on the vast personalized data we've accumulated over the years. After all, experience is the best teacher, right?

Sort of. We would go a step further: Experience is not the best teacher;

---

23. FYI: Tigger is a sanguine; Rabbit is a choleric; Pooh is a phlegmatic; Eeyore is a melancholic.

evaluated experience is.[24] What's the difference? Mainly, input. Finding someone to walk and talk with you through your experiences is helpful. Questions, observations, and a shared hunch or two can go a long way in evaluating what and why God has done something in our lives. The worse thing in the world is to be limited to our own perspective; involving others in our processing can help us catch themes and create theories we might not otherwise have on our own.

How have your experiences shaped you? One way to begin figuring this out is to draw a time line of your life and chart the significant events, people, places, lessons, and Scriptures that have been part of your history. As you plot your past, try to identify themes and ask yourself how you see those themes playing out in the present or continuing into the future. You might also randomly pick out one or more events and write out a couple of pages about what you remember about them, detailing what you thought, felt, said, and did. Then, after you've done some of this, pick someone you trust, grab some coffee, and talk about it.

Of all the variables we've mentioned (spiritual gifts, heart, abilities, personality), our experiences make up the one category we seem to be able to influence the most (revealing the tantalizing mystery of our responsibility and God's sovereignty). While we can't necessarily speak to what spiritual gifts or heart God has given us or really determine the natural abilities we have or the personality we've been given, there is a sense that we can affect the direction of our lives significantly if only we'd just try some new things and evaluate our experiences. And that's exciting.

These five categories are by no means exhaustive, and they fluctuate a bit in each of us, depending on the circumstances and people in our lives. Nevertheless, they do give us perspective into who we are and what we do. As we know ourselves and how God made us, we can continue becoming the kind of people the Lord intends us to be: Children of God first, doing all that we were created to do; and servants of God second, serving God and others.

---

24. I (Craig) am thankful to Paul Stanley, who taught Jack McQueeney, who taught me this truth.

Here's Mud in Your Eye

Knowing where we came from and how God has made us in the midst of the journey helps us trace the patterns in our lives within God's greater story. We gain perspective on how we live now as we recognize how others before us have struggled and succeeded, and how God has been faithful in the midst of it all.

Viewing our existence in light of where we're headed—our future eternity—helps our outlook on life as well. The Bible describes the culmination of this reclamation project at various times, most extensively in the book of Revelation. Revelation tells of the final defeat of Satan and the complete rule of Christ on earth as well as the glory and reign of all the saints, praising God and participating in a sinless society. This will extend throughout eternity and will be the best thing that has ever happened to us. (This is a serious understatement, but we can't describe it adequately.)

In the story of John 9:1-12, the man on the side of the road who was born blind knew that, in light of eternity, having a little mud in his eyes was a small price to pay to see Jesus.[25] Christ's actions of spitting in the dirt and rubbing mud in the man's eyes probably seemed strange and confusing, but the man's identity—who he was and who he would be from that point forward—were both changed as a result of Jesus' interest in and intention for his life.

The same can be true for us. We need to allow Jesus to open our eyes with the mud oozing within our existence in order to see our current situation in a broader context. If we do, we will see a greater vision for our lives, not a lesser one. We might better understand that we were created for a unique purpose by a loving God who has an amazing—if sometimes confusing—plan for our lives. God has made us in his image to have a relationship with him

25. I (Doug) have a friend who blew off both of his hands at the wrist with a pipe bomb when he was nineteen. Of course he'd love to have his hands back. But he'd tell you that this trauma was what turned him to Christ in the first place, and because of that he'd never trade what happened for a future with hands but without Jesus.

and others so we can work out our callings for the betterment, the *shalom*,[26] of the world. This understanding could change our identity forever.

Ideas of Things to Do

- Take your calling seriously. Do what you feel called to do with a sense of the importance of your contribution to the world in that area. If you are especially gifted in art, for example, pursue it with excellence. Many times we Christians produce substandard art because we aren't pushed to excel. Allow yourself to be sharpened and do your best.

- In your work and art, be real. We don't need the sugary Christianese that is so pervasive. Be honest with your struggles. Open up and let the world know that we don't have all the answers and don't live perfect lives. Talk and write about—and even paint—your pain, your defeats, your wonderings, your inner life. Christians don't have to be viewed as hypocrites but can be seen as real people who have a trustworthy and safe place to go with their hurts.

- Reconnect with your creativity. We all have something we can do to express the creative heart God has given us. Maybe it's something like painting, poetry, prose, music, or sculpting. Or you can be artistic in other areas. Organizing, decorating, showing mercy, and offering hospitality can all be creative. We can use our talents in the world in such a way that shows our Father as a Creator.

- Buy some art and display it in your home. Not something you can buy from a magazine, but something you picked out from an art show or had commissioned by one of your friends. It is uniquely

---

26. *Shalom,* literally "peace" in Hebrew, is the way things are supposed to be. Some characteristics of *shalom* are justice, rightness, holiness, goodness, and respect. You can read more about the *shalom* of God in Cornelius Plantinga Jr.'s book *Not the Way It's Supposed to Be* (Grand Rapids: Eerdmans, 1996).

satisfying to make an exchange of money and art with the artist himself, an experience you must take advantage of when you can.

- Don't allow your church to glorify and mystify "ministry" and brush off "secular" jobs. A biologist or letter carrier has just as much of a mission as a pastor or an overseas missionary.

Character cannot be developed in ease and quiet.
Only through experience of trial and suffering
can the soul be strengthened, ambition inspired,
and success achieved.

—HELEN KELLER, from Helen Keller's journal

A man's character is his fate.

—HERACLITUS

Character

One of our favorite individuals in the Bible is David. Here was a passionate man who lived life to the fullest, sometimes messed things up, and still in the end was called "a man after [God's] own heart" (Acts 13:22) because his *character*—his motivations, longings, and values—reflected the purposes of God.

For instance, in the story of David and Goliath, we read of a boy with rash behavior and staggering emotion who believed his God was bigger than the bad guy taunting him on the other side of the hill. When this boy grew up, King Saul threw spears at him while David played the harp, and yet David didn't retaliate when he had the opportunity. Later in his life, David cast the vision and made preparations for his son Solomon to build the Lord's temple. He wrote songs that expressed his heart—songs of hope, despair, discouragement, lament, thanksgiving, and deep, deep theology. He wept and wailed at the death of his son Absalom even though Absalom tried to kill him and to some degree succeeded in taking away the kingdom of Israel from David.

David also lusted, committed adultery, killed a man, and took that man's wife for his own. This—all this—was David. The very passion we admire as one of David's greatest strengths was also one of his greatest weaknesses. Yet his character grew strong as he continually turned to and sought after God.

Like David, we need to recognize that while our *passion*—our zest and zeal for life—may indeed be what takes us to great heights, our *character* is what will keep us from falling over the cliff in the process of getting there. Like David's, our passion can be wild and messy at times, not to mention so unmanageable that it gets us into trouble if we're not careful. So the intentional development of character in our twenties is crucial because this moral fiber is often the only thing that can bring balance to our motives and our actions.

Titus 2:11-12 says that the gospel, not our own grunts and groanings, leads us in this character transformation: The gospel "teaches us to say 'No' to ungodliness and worldly passions, and to live self-controlled, upright and godly lives in this present age." This gospel-changed good character brings balance to our decisions and deeds, brings our passions in line with Scripture, and gives God the credit by allowing him to shape our lives for his glory and not our own. A person who embraces the gospel with intention will grow in character. And it is this character that can reflect the very heart of God.

A multitude of character qualities are worthy of discussion: mercy, forgiveness, kindness, compassion, patience, goodness, self-control, joy, peacefulness, gentleness, and meekness, just to name a few (see Galatians 5 and Matthew 5–6). The next four chapters will look at four of the character qualities that are important to think about especially in our twenties: humility, integrity, teachability, and faithfulness.

Let the discussion begin.

CHAPTER THREE

Humility

OVERCOMING THE TYRANNY OF SELF

Pride is preoccupation with one's accomplishments and one's failures.
—JIM DOWNING, "Dealing with the Guilt of Your Past"

When a proud man thinks he is humble, his case is hopeless.
—THOMAS MERTON, *New Seeds of Contemplation*

Returning to college for my sophomore year, I (Craig) nervously opened the door, anxious to meet my new roommate. Didn't only losers roll the dice and go potluck their second year out? Doug and I had talked on the phone once over the summer, but we had yet to meet. And although we had each inferred from our few conversations that we were both Christians, who knew whether that would be enough to be good roommates?

Since Doug had unpacked but wasn't in the room, I surveyed my new roomie's side of our "cell." A little handmade sign that Doug had taped to the top of his desk stood out to me. The sign read in big block letters "HUMILITY" and just below in smaller letters was the reference "Philippians 2:3-4."[1] I later found out that Doug wanted to work on this character trait that year, and in the context of our little eight-by-eight dorm room, I soon discovered I needed to as well.

It was God's providence that Doug and I were thrown together so early in

---

1. "Do nothing out of selfish ambition or vain conceit, but in humility consider others better than yourselves. Each of you should look not only to your own interests, but also to the interests of others."

our twenties. Three years of living together provided many "opportunities" to identify just how arrogant and selfish we each could be as well as to help each other begin to overcome some of those traits. As we talked and thought about our humility (or lack thereof), what we found became a measure of—not a means to—our maturity. We needed each other to gauge how far we still had to go in the area of humility, but sometimes (and again through each other) we caught glimpses of how far we'd come as well, and that was good.

Perhaps you've already realized that at some point in our twenties— whether as a new roommate, a new employee, a newlywed, or a new parent— our default mind-set of "It's all about me" has to shift to "It's about me—but it's more about _____." True, some self-focus in our twenties is to be expected—we're making decisions about the future, trying to figure out who we are in new roles, thinking through what others are expecting of us. The danger comes when self-focus turns into self-infatuation and we use this pride of life to justify acting selfishly and arrogantly, a trap that can be more than easy to fall into.

Pride Comes Before the Fall (and After It, Too)

Pride goes back to before the beginnings of our human existence. In a probable reference to the fall of Satan,[2] the Scriptures record in Isaiah 14:12-15 how Lucifer—the most beautiful angel in heaven[3]—chose in his pride to set himself apart from God, and God cast him out of heaven before humans were even created:

---

2. "As Isaiah is describing the judgment of God on the king of Babylon (an earthly, human king), he then comes to a section where he begins to use language that seems too strong to refer to any merely human king.... It would not be uncommon for Hebrew prophetic speech to pass from descriptions of human events to descriptions of heavenly events that are parallel to them and that the earthly events picture in a limited way. If this is so, then the sin of Satan is described as one of pride and attempting to be equal to God in status and authority." (Wayne Grudem, *Systematic Theology: An Introduction to Biblical Doctrine* [Grand Rapids: Zondervan, 1994], 413.)

3. See also Ezekiel 28:12-15.

How you have fallen from heaven,
    O morning star, son of the dawn!
You have been cast down to the earth,
    you who once laid low the nations!
You said in your heart,
    "I will ascend to heaven;
I will raise my throne
    above the stars of God;
I will sit enthroned on the mount of assembly,
    on the utmost heights of the sacred mountain.
I will ascend above the tops of the clouds;
    I will make myself like the Most High."
But you are brought down to the grave,
    to the depths of the pit.

Picking up where Isaiah's account leaves off, Genesis tells us stories of the trappings of pride, beginning with the deception of Adam and Eve by the then-fallen Satan. As we know, Adam and Eve threw us into dire straits by representing us in their first sin and putting us out of whack in our relationship to God, to each other, and even with ourselves. Like Lucifer, they pridefully wanted to be their own authority and make their own choices, so they did—with implications that we still reel from today. Pride continued to show itself with Cain and Abel and with the people of Noah's day until God brought about the great flood.

After the flood, in Genesis 9:1, God told the people again they should scatter and go out to fill the earth. But in Genesis 11 we read that the people instead wanted to gather together to build a city with a tower—a really big tower. What's the big deal about this? We see the problem more clearly when we look at the specifics of Genesis 11:4:

1. *"Come, let us build ourselves a city, with a tower that reaches to the heavens."* The people wanted to build something impressive that would somehow give them access to heaven and, as one commentator writes, would "serve as a

staircase for the gods to come down from heaven into their temple and into their city."[4] From reading Genesis 9:1, we know that this was not what God had in mind.

2. "So that we may make a name for ourselves." The builders wanted to connect their name, their status, and their identity with the place they were building. The word and concept of *name* connotes "fame and progeny,"[5] and thus these people were seeking to find significance and meaning in their own achievements.

3. "And not be scattered over the face of the whole earth." As we have seen, this is exactly the opposite of what God had commanded them to do. They would never be in obedience to God if they hunkered down and didn't spread out. These people were afraid of a loss of place if they obeyed God, and so they found their solution in building a city and creating their own.

So what did God do? In Genesis 11:5-8 we see God undo all the things the people had done. It's as if the tower was so puny and pitiful that God had to stoop down with a microscope to see it.[6] He thwarted the plans of the people, frustrated their name building, and did the very thing they feared most—*scattered* them so they had to *rely* on him alone for meaning and security and not on their own efforts and reputation.

What does any of this have to do with us in our twenties? Like the Babel builders, most of us are looking for a way to stand out from the crowd. We want to make a name for ourselves. But that's not really how names work, for things and people don't name themselves; we receive names from others.

My (Doug's) three-year-old friend Nathan Brown calls his grandmother by the strange (and somewhat disturbing) name "Bugah." She loves it and wouldn't dream of changing it. She even has it emblazoned on her RV— "Bugah." Because Nathan gave her the name, she cherishes it. Contrast this

---

4. Bruce K. Waltke, *Genesis: A Commentary* (Grand Rapids: Zondervan, 2001), 179.
5. Waltke, *Genesis,* 179.
6. "This figurative usage implies no limitation on God's omnipotence, for the divine 'descent' presupposes prior knowledge of human affairs from on high, and God's subsequent counteraction unqualifiably exhibits His absolute sovereignty." (Waltke, *Genesis,* 83.)

with another grandmother I know who doesn't want to be called anything connected with grandmothering. Thus names like Nana, Gram, Grammie, and Granny were all tossed out, and she makes her grandkids call her "Honey" instead, which seems sort of pathetic and all about her. Naming herself reveals her insecurities.

Which names do you desire to be called? Is it Artist or Athlete or Beautiful or Life of the Party or Needing Attention or Always There When Someone Needs Me? If we understand how sinful we are and have received Christ's redemption, then God has already given us a name. We have a new identity—Christian—and no one but God can name us that.

Why then would we want to create other names for ourselves that contradict the name God has already given us? Who knows? But we'll be tempted to do so, and when we are, God will do the same thing he did at the time of Babel. When he scattered the people, he set them back on the course he wanted for them. His judgment was not only just but gracious, because it prevented them from moving farther away from him.

The Jesus Condition

Self-interest taints everything we do. Vanity—who we are and how we look being who we are—can easily consume us. Even our strengths and talents can become weaknesses and liabilities when we take credit for our successes and rely more on ourselves than on God.

We can observe this personal-preoccupation phenomenon in many little ways. How often do you think about how you look? what you're wearing? what your hair looks like? How do you handle conversations about things you don't especially care about? Do you listen and try to learn, or do you attempt to change the subject? When you meet new people, what do you want them to know about you? Do you engage in one-upmanship where every story begets another?

Getting married and having kids are two of the biggest blows to preoccupation with self that we've experienced. They don't make you instantly humble, but they help you see that the universe that once revolved around you is going to get much more complicated when a spouse and children enter your orbit. Make no mistake, we are important as individuals—incredibly so! But we are not the center of the universe.

Our culture tells us that unless we promote ourselves, we won't be important and we won't be noticed. As a result, we pursue higher positions and lust after acceptance. Like the two-year-olds we all once were, we want what we want. This is the human condition—we are consumed by self from birth.

But a different condition exists as well: the Jesus condition. Many people in the Bible demonstrated humble hearts,[7] but Jesus not only shows us his humility, he also gives us hope and strength to be humble.

While we could retrace Jesus' entire life, recounting the numerous ways he served us, let's concentrate on just one example: Jesus' last night before his death on the cross. In the Upper Room, Jesus consecrated the Passover meal. Then he did something else. Jesus showed his love for his disciples in a real and tangible way: "Having loved his own who were in the world, he now showed them the full extent of his love" (John 13:1). What did he do? He washed their feet.

Remember that most people in New Testament times wore Birkenstocks (or at least some kind of biblical-times equivalent) all day, every day. Others walked barefoot most of the time. Although the rest of their bodies might have been relatively clean, their feet got incredibly dirty and stinky, so it was a gesture of hospitality for hosts to wash their guests' feet before a meal or a time together.

Considered one of the most menial and low-level tasks around, foot washing was a job reserved for the servants of the house. But instead of asking a servant to do what needed to be done, Jesus himself took on that task, illustrating to the disciples his servanthood. Jesus had before him the excruciating march to the cross, the pain of death, and the wrath of God laid on him for the sins of all people, yet he thought of his disciples and their needs. The disciples should have worshiped at *his* feet, and yet Jesus stooped so low as to wash *their*

---

7. For instance: Abraham, who gave Lot the choice land; David, who allowed Saul to persecute him; Daniel, who served the Babylonians faithfully.

feet. He served them despite who they were, the very men who would deny him and show their misunderstanding about his mission on earth. And in their number: Judas the betrayer. Jesus washed his feet too.

"A new command I give you: Love one another. As I have loved you, so you must love one another" (John 13:34), Jesus told the disciples. The truth Jesus demonstrated teaches us how to live: Humbly serve one another, wash the feet of the person next to us, love others despite situations in which it might not make much sense. Many of us have heard this story more times than we can count, but it still hasn't sunk in. Jesus served. He laid himself and his position aside to wash the feet of others.

In general, servanthood isn't a common character trait of people in their twenties. Humble people around us stand out. Our friend John Hatfield used to be in a fraternity at Kansas State University. He was a varsity cheerleader, a party guy, and a basic hell-raiser. When he came to faith in Christ during his last two years of college, John found his life changing in ways he hadn't expected.

The predatory climate in his fraternity house allowed upperclassmen to torment the freshmen pledges. John had every "right" to continue that cycle of senior privilege when it came to small tasks, respect, and hazing. But responding to the gospel and Jesus' call on his life, John soon found himself cleaning up the vomit of the pledges after parties, wiping their mouths, changing their clothes, and getting them into bed. He started caring for them and being their friend, something rather startling to them. He loved them and lived out Christ's example through Christ's power in his life. In his twenties John began to understand how Jesus' life and example could bring him to a place where he would willingly put his own agenda aside and humbly serve others in their need.

We don't become humble just because we want to. Only when we realize the love of Christ for us and respond to that love can we hope to change. Jesus gave up heaven—*heaven!*—to come to earth and live the perfect life for us, dying the death we deserved. Talk about humility and servanthood! While Jesus never set aside his position as the Son of God to do all of this, he also didn't constantly claim or demand all that was his due. Instead, he served, despite the fact that he:

Who, being in very nature God,

    did not consider equality with God something to be grasped,

but made himself nothing,

    taking the very nature of a servant,

    being made in human likeness.

And being found in appearance as a man,

    he humbled himself

    and became obedient to death—even death on a cross!

      (Philippians 2:5-8)

Our attitudes and actions in serving others should reflect the example of Jesus. This is a hefty assignment, but one that Jesus gives us grace to meet. And doing so requires a healthy amount of humility.

Striking a Balance of Evaluation

A lot of how we think about humility has to do with how we think, period. In Romans 12:3, Paul wrote, "For by the grace given me I say to every one of you: Do not think of yourself more highly than you ought, but rather think of yourself with sober judgment, in accordance with the measure of faith God has given you." It's interesting how Paul addressed the Romans: with grace. He did not presume perfection on his part or on the part of the Romans but recognized instead that the only way he could admonish his readers to judge themselves was with grace and not some form of harsh legalism.

While Paul encourages us not to think of ourselves more highly than we ought, he also says not to write ourselves off either. Instead, he admonishes us to evaluate ourselves with sober judgment and with the measure of faith that has been given us. Striking this balance is important, lest we become so full of ourselves that no one can stand us, or so hopeless that we become depressed. Odds are that none of us is any more amazing or awful than the next person, but depending on our means of assessment, we could easily come to believe we are either.

While Paul's words make sense as to how we are to appraise ourselves, most of us usually end up comparing ourselves to others, evaluating our worth based on how the comparison plays out. If we end up "better" than others based on our skewed and private set of criteria, we feel good about ourselves; if others seem better than we are, we go through the process again and again until we either come out victorious or give up, utterly defeated.

Consider a room full of new moms, for example. The delight on each mother's face can be seen for miles, and the preciousness of a child in his or her mother's eyes inspires Hallmark cards. But things can turn ugly pretty fast if, in the wrong spirit, these moms begin talking about whose baby has walked first or whose child was the first to utter something that sounded like "Da-da" or how this or that feeding regimen will add fifty points to Junior's IQ.

All of our kids have had their own development time line—some have walked or talked early, some late. Both of our wives would acknowledge that at times their self-worth has been wrapped up in being thought of as a great mom with an achieving child who exceeds the national average on every scale and test. But each baby eventually walked and talked, so who cares who did it first or last?

Perhaps you can't relate to that example. You're not a mom. You don't know any moms. Or the moms you know are perfectly adjusted. If that's the case, try imagining a room full of business professionals establishing a pecking order. Or think about how you feel when you park your Chevy Metro next to the SUVs and sports cars in your church parking lot. Or perhaps you crave negative attention, which may seem better than none at all, better than not being noticed by anyone.

Evaluating ourselves against others is rarely a good idea, but perhaps an even worse plan is comparing ourselves with only ourselves (see 2 Corinthians 10:12). While this may seem a little silly, it is unfortunately how many people—especially those in their twenties—tend to live. I (Craig) can convince myself of just about anything, regardless of whether or not it's true. What makes this especially dangerous for me is that my melancholic tendencies can draw me into an emotional funk faster than you can say *Eeyore*.

For instance, on my thirtieth birthday I had planned to take the day off from work, head to a coffee shop, read my Bible, and spend a good couple of hours writing about the fact that I was no longer a twentysomething. While turning thirty was semiexciting, it was also ultradepressing. To quote Lorne Sanny, former president of The Navigators, when I once asked him what turning thirty was like for him: "It was the most depressing day of my life because I had been alive for so long and had accomplished so little." I felt very much the same way and was planning to write about and process some of this at length that day.

As it worked out, Maddie, my oldest daughter (then two years old), woke up superearly that morning and wouldn't go back to sleep. I got out of bed, took her downstairs, and sat down with her to watch the last half of the animated movie *The Prince of Egypt*. When we came to the part where Moses drove his staff into the waters of the Red Sea, I lost it. Completely. Bawling my eyes out and physically convulsing as a result of my new thirty-year-old emotions, one thought kept running through my head: *That's what I want God to do with my life. That's how I want to be used.*

The movie continued, and the Israelites crossed the Red Sea, making it to safety just before the suspended ocean came crashing down upon the unsuspecting Egyptian army. I sat there, still crying and shaking, with Maddie rubbing my shoulder, not wanting her daddy to be sad. Just then Megan came down the stairs and slowly walked into the living room, trying to figure out why her two-year-old daughter was comforting her now thirty-year-old weeping husband. I pointed to the television and blurted out, "That's what I want God to do with my life. That's how I want to be used. But it will never happen because it never has in thirty years."

Now that wasn't true. It was true that I'm not Moses, but God *had* used me and done some significant things over the course of my thirty-year life. I had just lost touch with reality, dismissing what God *had* done and instead beating myself up with what I thought God *should have* done.

The lesson I learned that day was a strange but important one: My real self will never be a match for my ideal self. As Paul admonished the believers in Rome, sober judgment and a measure of faith make far better companions than personal pride in the process of evaluating oneself. If we focus on how we can't part the Red Sea or how God hasn't put us in front of a Red Sea to part, we may miss what God *is* doing in and through us. We can lose a sense of his work in our lives when we become too consumed with what we want that work to be.

True vs. False Humility

As you work toward an accurate and sober picture of yourself, you may be tempted to take on the appearance of humility without seeking to be truly humble. This false humility is almost worse than being overtly prideful.

My (Craig's) talented friend Ken Bradbury once showed me the difference between false and true humility. I wanted Megan to meet Ken and see one of his musicals, so one summer night we went to one of his performances at the community theater center. As usual, the show was amazing, and Megan and I went backstage to see him and tell him so. Ken came over and hugged us, happy that we had come to the performance. As he let go of me, I said, "Boy, Ken, the show was fantastic!" and then waited for him to say something to the effect of "Well, it wasn't me" or "Oh, it wasn't that good." But instead, without pausing or breaking eye contact, Ken simply smiled, nodded his head, and said, "Wasn't it, though? It *was* good. I'm really glad you came."

I was dumbfounded. Ken didn't pretend that the show wasn't good, nor did he attempt to downplay my compliment with some kind of self-demeaning comment that he secretly hoped I would amend with another remark of praise. (I would have tried all of these tactics.) Instead, he just humbly agreed, genuinely grateful that we had come to see the performance, and we had a great time talking about how God had enabled him to create the show. When Megan and I said good-bye, I remember thinking, *It takes maturity to be that humble.*

More mature than most of us, Ken had moved past either grandiose or dirt-licking thoughts of himself. He displayed neither pride nor false humility but accepted the assessment given by others as true because he knew and appreciated the gifts God had given him and was content with that. It was a good lesson for me on the difference between true and false humility.

I (Doug) probably need to reconstruct that HUMILITY sign and put it on my desk again. It's frustrating how elusive true humility is and how pervasive pride can be in my life. As I go through my day, I find that it's tempting to keep looking for subtle ways to promote myself to others. A simple turn of the conversation and voilà! I can appear to be humble and yet reveal something great about myself in the process.

For instance, twice a year I go to staff training with the other RUF (Reformed University Fellowship) campus ministers, and I walk into a room of better pastors, better preachers, better thinkers, and better husbands than I'll ever be. They are funnier, smarter, and wittier than I am. I sometimes think to myself, *RUF at OU has seventy-five students, but Auburn has three hundred.* That keeps me from rejoicing over the ministry at Auburn or the other ministries at my own campus for that matter. As a result, I may carry on a conversation with these men about their ministries, downplaying what is going poorly in my ministry, while all the time cringing inside at God's blessing of their ministries, wanting more of it for me. It drives me into myself and away from God's perspective about both me and the other ministers I'm comparing myself to.

Another way to check our humility quotient is to notice how we react and feel while we're being praised. Unlike Ken did in the illustration above, many of us will act as if we don't want the praise, yet all the while secretly craving more and more of it. The real test is when we do something we're proud of and no one notices at all. Do we make sure to bring it up, or can we be content to let it go, knowing that God knows, sees, and is proud of us, and that his praise is all we need?

We need to look to God in these things. This "looking up" will keep us from relating to each other in this wrongheaded way. Then we can genuinely rejoice with our neighbors, our family, and our coworkers when something great happens to them and not to us, instead of simply pretending to.

Taking Steps to Walk More Humbly

One October day while passing through Columbia and visiting Old Mizzou, I (Craig) took Megan to an old rock quarry just south of campus, a place I used to frequent as a student when I wanted to get uninterrupted time alone with God. The splendor of fall in the Midwest was in full bloom, and we were fortunate enough to be sitting on a rock cliff overlooking a small part of it.

It was a perfect autumn scene, complete with cool but not cold temperatures as well as a "soundtrack" of a running stream below and the call of a bird or two in the stereophonics of nature. The slightly overcast sky made the colors of the trees flame even more.

And yet, it was all dying—the leaves that is. All the color and the beauty were a result of the slow death of each leaf. As I sat there with Megan, I started thinking about how much that phenomenon reflects the Christian life. We are most beautiful, most attractive, most stunning on the outside when we are dying—to ourselves, our wants, our desires, our lusts, and our very natures on the inside that say, "Preserve! Preserve! Preserve!"

Jesus said that "unless a kernel of wheat falls to the ground and dies, it remains only a single seed. But if it dies, it produces many seeds" (see John 12:24). He also said that whoever wants to save his own life will lose it, "but whoever loses his life for me will save it" (Luke 9:24). It's a paradox that in dying we receive life. While we desperately want to win, we don't exactly like Jesus' methods. He says we win when we...lose. But as we die to ourselves and humbly allow God to build *his* tower and give us *his* name, we don't lose—we win! This expectation should get our eyes off ourselves and onto the One who changes everything about us, who gives us these crazy ideas as well as the means to fulfill them.

At some point we have to realize that we are sinners who have come to Christ with nothing to offer but our sin. He takes our sin because he is gracious and merciful and loves us. He adopts us as his children, freeing us to live lives of meaning and purpose. Those are all actions outside us. God has transformed us, and he is still in the process of doing so: "Being confident of this, that he who began a good work in you will carry it on to completion until the day of Christ Jesus" (Philippians 1:6).

Walking humbly also means we truly look out for the needs of others above our own. If we do this, we can have an amazing impact on our peers, not so much because of our gifts, but simply because of our genuine interest in others at this time of our lives. Because this stage of life can be such a self-focused time, we will stand out if we choose to step out of our self-enamored lives and success strategies to instead champion the needs and interests of others.

Paul noticed two such others-focused people. In Philippians 2:19-30, Paul commended two colaborers of his, Timothy and Paul's messenger Epaphroditus. Why the commendations?

Paul said of Timothy: "I have no one else like him, who takes a genuine interest in your welfare" (verse 20), and "Timothy has proved himself, because as a son with his father he has served with me in the work of the gospel" (verse 22). Timothy's authentic—not obligatory—concern for others set him apart, and he "proved himself" by humbly serving.

About Epaphroditus, Paul said: "For he longs for all of you and is distressed because you heard he was ill" (verse 26). He instructed the Philippians to "Welcome him [Epaphroditus] in the Lord with great joy, and honor men like him, because he almost died for the work of Christ, risking his life to make up for the help you could not give me" (verses 29-30). Even when Epaphroditus was sick, he was worried that others were troubled because he might be a burden. Though ill, Epaphroditus risked his life and almost died trying to make up for the encouragement and support the Philippians were unable to give Paul in Rome.

As we look away from ourselves and toward the needs of others, we will find a strength we did not know we had. As we seek to make our lives a blessing instead of a burden to others, we will find satisfaction we previously did not know. Without Christ this is impossible, but with him, he develops our character as we grow in humility. This new way of living will enable us to make a name for ourselves, one that God will gladly bestow upon us in addition to the one he has already given each of us as his children. That second name? Humble.

Ideas of Things to Do

- Don't take credit for things you didn't do.
- Serve by volunteering to do jobs you don't like.

- Give thanks for the people who regularly do the jobs you don't like to do. Show them that you appreciate them.
- Write thank-you notes to people when they do nice things for you.
- Submit yourself to the elders of your church.
- Realize that you don't know everything, and learn humbly from everyone.
- Allow God to lift you up in due time—don't take matters into your own hands.
- Listen to people—especially those who love you—when they offer critique and criticism.
- Learn a new skill. It will remind you that you can't do everything well.

CHAPTER FOUR

Integrity

LIVING OUT WHO WE ARE

Who steals my purse steals trash...but he that filches from me my good
name...makes me poor indeed.

—WILLIAM SHAKESPEARE, *Othello*, Act 3, Scene 3

The pursuit of integrity is never the pursuit of perfection
but of who I am and of what I can do.

—BILL THRALL, *The Ascent of a Leader*

An amazingly powerful scene ends Arthur Miller's scripted version of the movie *The Crucible*. In it, an innocent John Proctor faces a dilemma: Sign a confession stating that he worships the devil and live, or refuse to sign and hang publicly with four others. Proctor, with his wife at his side and pen in his hand, thinks long and hard about this excruciating decision. Hesitantly, he signs...but then he quickly grabs the paper in hopes of wadding it up and throwing it away. "There," he says. "I did it. I signed. You saw me. What more do you need? I confess."

Unfortunately for Proctor, the ministers demand the parchment back so they can publicly post his confession of practicing witchcraft on the church door for all to see. Proctor argues with them for a minute, not understanding why the public needs to be informed of his private decision. After making no headway, Proctor finally gives the signed parchment to the ministers—only to grab it back once more and rip it to shreds before their eyes.

Warning that the destroyed parchment would not be considered a true confession, the ministers plead with Proctor to sign a new parchment. Continuing to tear the original parchment to bits, Proctor passionately cries, "But it's my name, and I shall have no other!" Immediately they arrest him, take him to the gallows, and John Proctor hangs as an innocent man, quoting the Lord's Prayer just before the wood creaks and the rope stretches. The screen fades, the credits roll, the end.[1]

Whoa.

What's in a name? And why did John Proctor care about his so much that he was willing to die rather than desecrate it? Why has someone's name on a piece of paper traditionally been a means of legally binding an agreement made between two separate parties? When we sign our names to the top of tests, scrawl them across the bottom of our checks, or carefully write them on marriage licenses, what do our names attached to these documents really mean? Do they mean anything at all?

Our names are important because they give us an *identity*. Johnny Cash sang about "A Boy Named Sue," whose name changed his life in every way. Some of you may use your middle name because you feel it fits you better. Or you may have adopted your nickname as your own. Or you may hate your high-school nickname and hope we never find out what it is.

Our names stand for our *reputations*. What do people think when they hear the name Craig Dunham or Doug Serven? What do people think of when they hear your town or school or company or church spoken of in conversation? What does your name represent to others, and are you satisfied with that?

Our names carry *power*. When we name-drop, we're using the power of someone else's name in some way to represent our own. If we do this carelessly or lie about it, we are posing as something other than who we are.

As we consider our names, we need to remember the warning of John Proctor that indeed they are ours, and we shall have no other. We should tell the truth and not lie—or our names will carry "liar" on them. We should be honest and not deceitful ("shady character"). We should not overpromise and

---

1. *The Crucible,* directed by Nicholas Hytner, screenplay by Arthur Miller (Twentieth Century Fox, 1996).

then underdeliver ("slacker"). We should let our yes be yes and our no be no (Matthew 5:37), or we will inherit the label "can't trust him or her." All of this is supposedly everything we needed to know and learned in kindergarten, but many of us could use a refresher course in the fine art of establishing and protecting the integrity of our good names.

Integrity Is Not Perfection

We all know that each of us is just as messed up as the next person. Few of us would deny the taint of sin in our lives. But some of us can talk about it, and some of us can't. Integrity—living out who we are—is the key to coming face to face with what we know to be true about ourselves.

It's important to understand that when we talk about integrity we're talking about a *characteristic*—not a *competency*—of the Christian life. Here's a good way to think about this: When naval captains speak of a ship's integrity, they aren't speaking of what propels the ship, but what keeps it afloat. Integrity in our lives cannot be "done"; it can only be described. We cannot live a life of integrity on the outside without the reality of integrity on the inside. A car only runs when there's gas in the tank; a child only grows when there's food in his or her stomach. We need to know the truth about who we are and aren't in order to live out integrity.

It can be tempting (especially in our twenties) to fall into the legalistic trap of wanting to be *perfect* rather than wanting to grow to be a person of integrity. We begin to think that if we look good on the outside surely we must be good on the inside. This incongruent existence quickly becomes the breeding ground for hypocrisy, bringing with it guilt, frustration, and exhaustion. Living with integrity gives us permission to make known the desperate need we have for the grace of God, allows us to receive grace from God and others, relieves us of our guilt, and redeems our lives in the process.

The artist Vincent van Gogh avoided the temptation to present himself as perfect and instead presented himself as he was.[2] Here was a man who

2. Thanks to Russ Ramsey for this illustration and the following thoughts on Matthew.

shared his heart (and also a part of his ear). The details are a bit fuzzy, but we know this: Van Gogh loved a woman, and one night he was in such a daze that he decided an ear would make a lovely present for her. So he cut one off (or at least part of it), put it in a jar, and, hopeless romantic that he was, took it to her. Happy Valentine's Day! Later his brother found him bleeding from his head and took him back to his room to heal, presumably lecturing him all the way about how flowers or chocolates are always appropriate, but diamonds are a girl's best friend.

Imagine the shame van Gogh must have felt when he was permanently minus an ear, a constant reminder of that one night of poor judgment. And yet van Gogh created two or three paintings from that time period in which he reveals his bandaged ear for everyone to see. In essence, he was saying, "This is who I am, disfigured and all. I am sorry, I am guilty, I am not amused, but here I am." He could have easily painted the other side of his head to hide his disfigurement, but for some reason he didn't. He was honest with himself and with the viewer of his self-portrait.

Now being that honest is hard for us. We may have glaring wounds, but we tend to hide them from others, showing our "good" side whenever possible. But like van Gogh, could we muster enough courage to reveal our ears (or the absence of one of them), showing our wounds and bandages despite being scared that others will think less of us or treat us differently as a result? Integrity means living out who we are.

Telling on Ourselves

In Matthew 9:9-13, we read the story of Jesus' call to Matthew.[3] In his gospel, Matthew began the story of his own conversion by identifying himself as a tax collector. In other words, like most tax collectors in his day, he was a thief, a

---

3. Matthew wrote his book to tell us about the gospel. He included himself (in third person, as was the custom of the day) to show how he, too, was affected by the gospel Jesus proclaimed, that he (just as we are) was a more wicked and despicable sinner than he could ever imagine, and yet at the same time he was more loved and accepted than he ever thought possible because Jesus Christ lived and died in his place.

cheat, and a self-serving scoundrel. But to Christ, Matthew was acceptable, even valued.

So Matthew told on himself. In a sense, he repented with godly sorrow. He confessed that he was a tax collector, that he hung out with tax collectors and sinners, and that he had no reason for deserving a relationship with Jesus—except one: Jesus came to call sinners to repentance.

Matthew showed integrity by not hiding the fact that he was a sinner. And so, as we read his words, we discover a man who had been changed by the love of God and took a moment to tell the story. Matthew seemed to be amazed that Jesus, knowing full well what kind of person Matthew was, still accepted and loved him.

Look at your own life for a minute. What do you do to keep people from knowing that you are a sinner? What do you use to hide yourself in false humility? What lies do you tell to paint yourself in a better light? And why do so many of us continue to hide the fact that we are sinners?

When we try to hide our sin, we are hiding the gospel from people. We are working to keep our need for Christ hidden from the eyes of others who need him just as much. Why do we do this? Because we can't believe—deep down believe—that Jesus would want to eat with sinners like us. Surely he'd rather have a meal with someone who looks much better than that, at least on the outside.

So go ahead—tell on yourself. We need to admit that we are the sinners we are. We need to be honest about the destruction we cause in our lives and in others' lives as we go about our ways and seek our own glory. We need to repent and turn to Christ for forgiveness and a new way of looking at things. And we need to try to become people who care about others before ourselves, who seek rightness in the world, and who commune with God and seek his ideals.

In integrity, we should also be willing to share our faults and struggles with others. This doesn't mean taking out a full-page ad in *USA Today* to share our deepest sins, but we can start by sharing with close friends or in a small group a specific sin we're dealing with or an attitude we have that is hardly humble. We should be willing to give testimony to God's work in our lives because he has sought us—sinners like us, can you believe it?!—to be his children. When we do, we relieve the burden of our secrets, our hypocrisy, and our false pretensions and are then free to be as unique and passionate as we can be. So tell on yourself soon and often, as it is the very thing that will give you life.

Julie and I (Doug) began to tell on ourselves and move toward integrity when we received some Christian counseling in our late twenties. With suspicion and tentative steps, I walked into the counselor's office as a disapproving critic waiting to be won over but doubting it would ever happen. What took place over the next few months opened up our marriage and helped us realize what things were making us angry, hurt, and disconnected from each other. Some of our issues were extremely personal as we both told stories and shared our hearts with each other and our counselor.

It was a great experience to be so freely listened to, taken seriously, understood, and accepted. Through counseling we better understood who we were and how we affected each other. We moved toward integrity by being honest with our hurts and hopes, our despair and dreams. If we hadn't delved into those areas, we may have been able to manage our lives on the outside, but we would have been missing out on something greater.

Just as Julie and I did in our counseling sessions, we all need to dig in and talk about who we truly are and how we got that way. These lines penned by Charlie Peacock and Douglas McKelvey hit hard as we examine ourselves:

I've run my ship aground on the rocks of the soul
There's no lie like independence; there's no demon like control
I've fanned the burning embers till my house was on fire
There's no parody like power; there's no fever like desire
I've drained the wine of darkness to the dregs of deceit
There's no drug as strong as pride; there's no blindness like conceit
I've railed against a mountain with a pickax and a file
There's no minefield like presumption; there's no death wish like denial
There's no gunshot like conviction; there's no conscience bullet proof
There's no strength like utter weakness; there's no insult like the truth

I've adjusted my prescription till I couldn't trust my vision

There's no killer like convenience; there's no sickness like omission

I've amended resolutions and resisted explanation

There's no trap door like emotion; there's no pit like reputation

There's no cancer like ambition; there's no cure like crucifixion[4]

We need the courage to open those rooms to who we are and let some fresh air in. This moves us toward the integrity Christ calls us to. We don't necessarily have to go to counseling to open these doors and move toward wholeness. We need to talk to the people who love us no matter what and *let* them love us by confessing our sins to them and giving them the opportunity to show us grace.[5]

Rethinking Performance

Puritan John Owen said, "The greatest sorrow and burden you can lay on the Father, the greatest unkindness you can do to Him is not to believe that He loves you."[6] Now before this quote turns into yet another reason to feel guilty about just how much you fail—Stop! You are trying to perform again. And that's the problem. Sometimes we get so caught up in trying to obey God that we decide we have to do more than what is expected of us to achieve integrity. Our godly desires turn into human performance instead of a longing to know God's love more deeply.

Job's friend, Eliphaz, is a good example of this. In an attempt to comfort Job after his family calamities and catastrophic new dermatology, Eliphaz recounted to Job the many ways he had helped others through instruction, by strengthening feeble hands and faltering knees (Job 4:3-4), and by supporting

---

4. Charlie Peacock and Douglas Kaine McKelvey, "Insult Like the Truth," copyright © 1996 Sparrow Song/River Oaks Music Company/BMI. All rights reserved by EMI Christian Music Publishing. Used by permission.
5. This is what James 5:16 is all about.
6. John Owen, *Communion with God,* ed. R. J. K. Law (Edinburgh, Scotland: Banner of Truth Trust, 1991), 13.

those who stumbled. Then Eliphaz did exactly what each of us is so easily given to do—he asked a question that stemmed from his desire for personal justification: "Should not your piety be your confidence and your blameless ways your hope?" (Job 4:6). Eliphaz didn't get it.

We might begin the Christian life with the gospel as our righteousness and our salvation, but then slowly start to offer up our good deeds as pleasing to God. We put aside the Cross of Christ and present to God our pious attempts at "living right." Because we have convinced ourselves that everything is now dependent on us, we start to hide our failures because they are a judgment against the inadequacies that we all live with as humans. And yet God will not allow us to walk down this road forever because he is just and cares for us too much.

Matthew 7:15-23 is one of those scary Bible passages in which Jesus tells it like it is: "Not everyone who says to me, 'Lord, Lord' will enter the kingdom of heaven, but only he who does the will of my Father who is in heaven" (verse 21).[7] Jesus explains that he's talking about people who have done ministry in his name. They preached, they cast out demons, and they ministered. They were on the church leadership team. They went on mission trips. They volunteered for Vacation Bible School. They gave blood. They sang in the choir. They organized fund-raisers for the homeless. They led Bible studies. But external demonstrations do not prove integrity. Integrity is a question of the heart. Integrity means acting out of an understanding of God's grace, not out of a desire to perform.

Author Jerry Bridges has been particularly helpful to me (Craig) in this area of trying to understand and live in grace. Not only have his books encour-

---

7. "They have confessed me with their tongue, and think they have done everything right: even now, the confession of my Name may be heard rolling from their lips, but I shall get up and answer them, that all their profession is empty and untrue. What does Christ's confession [against these false confessors] consist of? A declaration that He has never counted them amongst His people, even at the time when they were boasting that they were pillars of the Church. So He tells them to be off from Him, who for a time, with fake credentials, had robbed Him of the possession of His house." John Calvin's commentary on Matthew, quoted in *Commentaries,* ed. David W. Torrance and Thomas F. Torrance, 23 vols. (Grand Rapids: Eerdmans, 1960–), 240.

aged me but we've met for lunch every now and then. One day while we were eating subs, Jerry said something that significantly changed my perspective on performance: "God is indeed a God of performance, but Jesus performed in our place. The gospel is for sinners, and that's exactly what we are. We just have to remind ourselves."

Jerry went on to say that there are four different philosophies we can adopt concerning our walk with God:

1. It's "all God," which relieves us of any responsibility for our spiritual growth after we have trusted Jesus.
2. It's "all me," which places the burden of growth completely on our shoulders.
3. It's "part God, part me," which leaves us trying to figure out how much of each part of our sanctification is God's and how much is ours. (This is the one I was trying to live by at the time.)
4. It's "all God, all me," which places all reliance for my sanctification on God and all effort for my trust in him and his work in my life. (This is the one I'm now trying to live by.)

Brennan Manning, in his book *The Ragamuffin Gospel,* says much the same thing about performance and the philosophies that surround it:

> Many of us are haunted by our failure to have done with our lives what we longed to accomplish. The disparity between our ideal self and our real self, the grim specter of past infidelities, the awareness that I am not living what I believe, the relentless pressure of conformity, and the nostalgia for lost innocence reinforces a nagging sense of existential guilt: I have failed. This is the cross we never expected, and the one we find hardest to bear.[8]

Manning goes on to say that Jesus is not surprised by our failures. In fact, he expects them more than we do. This, Manning argues, defines grace.

If Jesus really expects us to fail even more than we do, why don't *we* expect

---

8. Brennan Manning, *The Ragamuffin Gospel* (Sisters, Oreg.: Multnomah, 1990), 186.

to fail? Why do we allow our fear of rejection or humiliation to keep us from confessing our sins to God and to one another? Why do we think we can rise above this awful, inherited condition of sin on our own to somehow be different from every other person (except Jesus) who has walked the face of the earth?

With this in mind, we need to more freely admit our weaknesses, both to Christ and to others. Such confession keeps us from being deceitful and helps us become more honest. With true repentance in our hearts and more experience in offering it to God, we might better understand our own frailties and be able to admit our shortcomings. In fact, in our Christian lives, we should become better repenters—quicker to realize and turn away from our sins and make less of a fuss about going to Jesus for forgiveness.

To do this we need to talk to Jesus a lot and tell him how we're doing. Our prayers then reflect our dependence on Christ as we come to him, laying before his feet all our needs and all our triumphs. We also need to share with our friends the things that we're struggling with so they can help us turn our eyes toward Jesus. As we walk humbly, we depend more on Jesus and become more genuine in our actions with others, asking better questions and listening more deeply.

Only when we accept that we are sinners (according to Romans 3:23) does the prescription on the bottle of grace make sense. Only when we decide confession and not cover-up is the means to a better end do we begin to live in the light of who God has made us to be, for we are finally being truthful about who we really are, which is what living in integrity is all about. As television kitchen connoisseur Julia Child would say, following such a recipe always makes for great cooking.[9]

The Practice of Truth and the Presence of God

Think of two people who represent people of integrity to you. Does it seem that they have to work at it, always *trying* to be trusted, counted on, and taken seriously by others? No, they simply *are* trusted, counted on, and taken

---

9. We have no idea if she would really say this.

seriously by others. So what makes the difference between trying and being? And how would these people explain the difference to you if you asked them?

We would guess they would say they practice truth—biblical and otherwise—in living their lives. They don't overpromise and then underdeliver; they swear to tell the whole truth and nothing but the truth; they admit it when they're wrong. Their integrity shines out to the world.

We are drawn to people who display integrity, to people who can be trusted. Used-car salesmen don't exactly have that reputation—they'll tell you whatever you want to hear. Infomercials can't be trusted because everything looks wonderful in the right light and conditions. But real integrity—honesty, truthfulness, lack of hype—stands out in our day and age. As theologian and pastor Francis Schaeffer wrote in his book *The God Who Is There:* "In an age of relativity, the practice of truth, when it is costly, is the only way to cause the world to take seriously our protestations concerning truth."[10]

I (Doug) have a friend—I'll call him Chas—who recently told me about an affirming and surprising experience he had that got him thinking more about integrity. Chas had worked at a summer camp in California as a staff volunteer. Out of the blue several years later, Chas received a phone call from a mother in Minnesota who was trying to help her daughter work through a problem with an older man. The girl was eighteen; he was forty-one, twice divorced, and pursuing her because he believed she was the "one" for him. Chas remembered the girl from that summer but had never met the mother, a fact she acknowledged when Chas answered the phone. After she identified herself, what floored Chas was her next comment: "Though I've never met you, my daughter has had nothing but good things to say about you and the way you treated her when she was in California. That's why I called—I thought I could trust you because of who she said you were."

Those words humbled Chas—and scared him to death. But as he worked through the situation with the mom and saw God work things out for the good, he felt grateful that somebody had noticed how he was trying to live his

10. Francis Schaeffer, *The God Who Is There* (Chicago: InterVarsity, 1968), 169.

life and that years later it led to an unexpected chance to minister to someone he had never met before in his life.

God uses our integrity to influence others for the sake of his kingdom and purposes. The prophet Amos said, "Seek good, not evil, that you may live. Then the LORD God Almighty will be with you, just as you say he is" (Amos 5:14). As we seek to incorporate God's truth into every aspect of our lives, we must remember that he delights in us as we represent him as his sons and daughters. This, more than anything else, should motivate us to pursue integrity—living out who we are because God has said he will be with us… just as we say he is.

Ideas of Things to Do

- Don't lie on your taxes.
- Don't pretend you're someone else to get something you want.
- Don't pretend you're someone else on the Internet.
- Pay people back when you borrow money from them.
- Follow through on tasks that have been assigned to you.
- Don't get addicted to things (not even coffee).
- Be honest with yourself and with others. Be real. Be vulnerable (when appropriate).
- Repent often.
- Keep your commitments even if it hurts. Hold yourself to them. Do not break them.

CHAPTER FIVE

Teachability

LEARNING TO LEARN FROM ANYONE

*In order to influence people, the artist must be constantly searching, so that
his work is a quest. If he has discovered everything and knows everything
and instructs people or deliberately sets out to entertain them, he has no
influence on them. Only when he is searching for the way forward, do the
spectator and the listener become one with him in his quest.*

—LEO TOLSTOY

Perhaps my greatest wisdom is the knowledge that I do not know.

—JOHN STEINBECK, *Travels with Charley*

Having zeal without knowledge is both exciting and problematic, sort of
like jumping out of an airplane without a parachute. In the same way,
thinking that we can figure out who we are without being willing to learn
from God, others, and life itself is a ride that will hurt in the end. The surest
way to avoid this hard landing? Learn to learn from anyone.

In a culture that wields knowledge as power and prizes information, it can
be difficult to learn from others, especially during a stage of our lives in which
we are so desperately trying to prove ourselves to those around us. And yet
teachability is an exercise in humility that usually involves having to say, "I
don't know." Rick Foster, author of *The Challenge* newsletter, agrees:

> The difference between learning and being taught is this: learning
> appeals to our pride and ego…being taught requires submission and

the acceptance of authority. Learning can end up filling in the space between our ears. But correction and discipline will not give up until there is life-change. It's the difference between information and transformation. God is never satisfied to fill our minds…He wants to radically alter our lives.[1]

I (Craig) began to learn about my own lack of teachability in college, just after I met students involved with the campus ministry of The Navigators. Doug had joined the group the semester before me and attended a student-led Bible study. I wasn't involved because of my time commitment with Marching Mizzou[2]—and because I wasn't that excited about learning anything from the Bible in a study taught by a peer.

One day Doug asked if I might be interested in seeing the latest thing he had learned in his study—the Wheel Illustration, a fairly simple tool used to evaluate the balance in our spiritual lives. While I had no desire to listen to him, my parents raised a courteous child, so I agreed to give Doug a little of my time. This was going to hurt.

As we sat in our dorm room, Doug took pencil and paper and began to draft the wheel. He wanted to practice what he had learned, but I was angry that he assumed I wanted to learn something from him. I shut down and said nothing, nodding my head obligatorily with the intention of getting this over as soon as possible.

While I can't recall how the time ended, I will never forget how silly I felt afterward that I couldn't learn a simple illustration from someone who cared about me and wanted me to grow as a Christian. I didn't want to learn from Doug because I was too proud to be taught by my roommate and peer. I don't know which was worse: the way I acted or the way I felt. I had been unteachable, and I was ashamed of my childishness.

The truth is, if we struggle with the idea of learning from "anyone," we run the risk of learning from no one. If people have to be of a certain age or

---

1. Rick Foster, *The Challenge*, 1 February 2001.
2. The University of Missouri's marching band. Mizzou-Rah!

background, have a certain kind of experience or ability, or hold some official position before we give them permission to speak into our lives, we will never allow anyone to teach us. We will always be evaluating the credentials of others instead of learning what God would have us learn from someone else.

This concept reminds me (Doug) of when our family was making popcorn strands for one of our Christmas trees a few years ago. Julie and I gave instructions to the kids, but Cal, who was four at the time, didn't really listen and dove right in. He discovered the process wasn't as obvious as he had thought, and he began to get frustrated as four-year-olds tend to do. Julie patiently told him that he needed to put the needle and thread down for a minute and listen to Mommy. He needed to be teachable or he wouldn't get it.

Our society values independence, and we all want to stand on our own eventually. But not only is complete independence an illusion and a myth, even if it were possible, it would be a detriment to real growth. We don't operate as individuals; we live in community. We didn't begin our culture; we're continuing in it. We need to appreciate those who have gone before us and those who stand around and with us, learning from all of them.

When we think there's nothing new worth hearing, that we've heard it all before, or that we don't need to hear it from someone who is our age or has roughly our same experience, we reflect our arrogance and unwillingness to learn. The Bible has quite a bit to say about this topic.[3] We'll boil down a few of these principles to this: Teachability is the cultivated aptitude to learn from anyone. When it comes to answering the question, Who am I? in our twenties, teachability is essential.

It's a Different World

The Jewish tradition of apprenticeship is one of the oldest forms of learning in the world, existing from the beginning of civilization itself. Greeks like Socrates, Plato, and Aristotle later passed on this concept of mentoring (named

---

3. See the book of Proverbs, for example.

for Mentor, who trained future kings) to their students.[4] Even Jesus received this type of education in his youth. In *Mentoring for Mission,* Günter Krallman writes:

> Undoubtedly, Joseph trained Jesus in this way [apprenticeship] too. Time and again during the countless hours they spent together in the workshop, Joseph would explain and demonstrate, while Jesus listened, observed, and imitated. Through close and extensive "with-ness" in the shared working environment, Jesus gradually advanced in knowledge, skill, and experience, until He became a proficient carpenter Himself.[5]

When Jesus began his public ministry at the age of thirty, he carried on this concept of apprenticeship in the training of his disciples.[6] He spent countless hours with them, answered questions, and sought to pass on to them a sense of mission, vision, and values.

Paul later picked up where Jesus left off. Having been tutored by Barnabas after his dramatic conversion experience, a more mature Paul sought to encourage and train Timothy, his "true son in the faith" (1 Timothy 1:2). After spending time with Timothy and his family in their home and building trust, Paul took Timothy with him on his travels, exposing him to a variety of new and exotic places, interesting people, and amazing experiences.

Nothing diminished Paul's developmental bias for Timothy. When they weren't together, Paul prayed for him; when Paul was imprisoned, he wrote Timothy letters filled with words of affection, theological truths, and practical advice. The worth and potential of the individual was key to Paul's thinking. In Paul's second letter to Timothy, Paul summed up his strategy of discipleship, encouraging Timothy to make it his own as well: "And the things you have heard me say in the presence of many witnesses entrust to reliable men who will also be qualified to teach others" (2:2).

---

4. In fact, much of our Western tradition of thought (not to mention architecture and art) came about as a result of the deep, frequent discussions these men had.
5. Günter Krallman, *Mentoring for Mission* (Hong Kong: Jensco, 1987), 26-7.
6. The Greek word for "disciple" is *mathetes,* which means "follower" or "learner."

What's the point? Learning used to be personal. It used to be thorough and slow. It used to be very, very intentional. And it seemed to work.

When the Renaissance dawned around the sixteenth century, however, universities were established, and people started to depend more on group environments than on one-on-one learning. That wasn't all bad, but it certainly put more of a burden on the student to learn than on the teacher to teach. Then the Industrial Revolution hit in the nineteenth century. Money was to be made, fathers went off to work in factories, and parents became increasingly less likely to instruct their children about occupations, beliefs, and daily life. Our modern construction of public schools and universities are a result of this continuing progression.

The trend away from one-on-one learning has continued. We now have unprecedented access to information through the Internet but little interest in applying what we find there. We rely heavily on the environments that "progress" has given us to replace human touch. Instead of looking to someone to model answers for us, we turn to computers, televisions, and media to give us information.

In 1986, New York University professor Neil Postman wrote a prophetic little book called *Amusing Ourselves to Death.* In the foreword he writes,

> What [George] Orwell feared were those who would ban books. What [Aldous] Huxley feared was that there would be no reason to ban a book, for there would not be anyone who wanted to read one. Orwell feared those who would deprive us of information. Huxley feared those who would give us so much that we would be reduced to passivity and egoism. Orwell feared that the truth would be concealed from us. Huxley feared that the truth would be drowned in a sea of irrelevance.[7]

Postman concludes that Huxley—not Orwell—was right. Today we find ourselves bobbing in a "sea of irrelevance." If we are to learn more than facts

---

7. Neil Postman, *Amusing Ourselves to Death* (New York: Penguin, 1986), vii.

during the course of our lives, we have to fight to do so because our culture and environment are not going to paddle with us toward that end.

Intention: Lining Things Up to Learn

If we are not self-motivated to learn for our own intellectual, emotional, and spiritual development, chances are we will not be on our way to becoming learners anytime soon.

Psalm 37:37 says, "Consider the blameless, observe the upright; there is a future for the man of peace." I (Craig) came across this verse just after I graduated from college and moved to Colorado Springs for my second summer at Eagle Lake, a Christian camp for kids. I was twenty-two, dirt poor, in debt, and set to move in with camp director Jack McQueeney, his wife, Shaunda, and their four kids in the fall. I wanted to ease into a new stage of life, save some money, and experience nine months in a Christian home that wasn't my own.[8] With Psalm 37:37 in mind, I set my mind and heart to the "consider and observe" setting, with the hope of growing into "a man of peace." This experience turned out to be one of the best encounters of my twenties.

What made it so good? Two things: Jack and Shaunda were ready to teach, and I (after several revealing experiences like the one with Doug) was ready to learn. Unfortunately, this dynamic of willing teacher and teachable pupil doesn't often naturally line up the right way. It takes shared desire, compatible personalities, convenient timing, and a sense of need. It takes intention, too. For instance, during that season of my life, I purposely cut off most things social so I would be able to eat all of my meals with the family. I spent all day Saturday working with Jack around the house, laying sod in the backyard,

---

8. Back in the late 1930s and early 1940s, Navigators founder Dawson Trotman and his wife, Lila, invited young men and women to live with them in their modest Los Angeles home for a period of months. The purpose of these accommodations was not as much communal as it was communicative, the idea being that aspects of biblical living could be passed on more effectively when life-on-life relationships were translated through life-on-life living arrangements.

cleaning the garage, and doing other general tasks. I helped Shaunda with laundry and dishes and watched the kids on Tuesday nights while she and Jack were at Bible study. A lot of work, you're thinking. But what did I get in return?

I got the McQueeney family living their lives in front of me. I was privy to parenting techniques, reasons behind financial decisions, and full-out arguments about the best way to handle situations that came up in their lives. I gained a more balanced perspective on money, time, ministry, and family than I had accumulated on my own. I learned how awful morning sickness can be (Shaunda was pregnant with their fourth child at the time) and how that was part of the joy and curse of creating life. I saw how to work biblical truths into daily routines and the true commitment it takes to really love someone else.

And through teaching me, the McQueeneys learned about themselves. In a weird way, they were teachable about teachability. They discovered more about who they were as a couple in their thirties by teaching me in my twenties. I would have learned nothing without making the decision to stay home and stick with the process, even when it got hard. The McQueeneys would have learned nothing about teaching these things had they not been secure in their marriage and committed to me enough to endure this invasion of their privacy. It was uncomfortable, unforgettable, and something we are all grateful for even today.

One thing Jack taught me was that, when it comes to any kind of learning, the burden of responsibility rests squarely on our shoulders. First Timothy 4:7 says the same thing: "train *yourself* to be godly" (emphasis added). As I learned in the McQueeney home, intention is the key to education.

In your job, living situation, or friendships, do you position yourself to learn from those who are a little older than you? Who are you seeking out for help among the elders and mentors in your church or family? Have you written off older generations as irrelevant, or are you asking them questions about decisions you may have to make in the future? Intentionally engaging others leads to teachability and reflects teachability, strengthening our character for both the present and the future.

Product and Process in Balance

Real learning doesn't just increase the sum of our knowledge, it expands our method of thinking. This development comes from being as interested in the trial as in the task of figuring things out. As we attempt to gather the *product* of answers, we can't miss the *process* through which those answers come.

People who recognize this balance soak up information from everything and everyone around them. A fictional character, Peekay, displayed this sort of teachability. Peekay grew up in the bush of South Africa. His nanny was Zulu, and his mentor was a German music professor/botanist. Peekay made friends everywhere he went. He wanted to squeeze everything out of the world around him, to learn from every experience, to live life to its fullest. Things were by no means always good—during his first years at school, he was picked on for being different since he was English and not Afrikaans like the rest of the boys. But as he left for a new life, he ran into Hoppie, a boxer who made a profound impact on Peekay. *"I had known him a little over twenty-four hours,"* said Peekay, *"yet he had managed to change my life.* He had given me the power of one—one idea, one heart, one mind, one plan, one determination. Hoppie had sensed my need to grow...he gave me hope" (italics added).[9] Peekay's learning wasn't simply from schoolbooks or seminars, but from his spongelike way of gleaning from every person and experience he encountered. He valued the process as well as the product.

Trying to find this balance between process and product in daily life can be difficult. A couple of years ago, Megan and I (Craig) were involved in a young couples' class at our church. The group was comprised largely of young believers and even younger marriages, and sometimes we felt out of place in the discussion because we didn't want to just figure things out as much as talk about the messy process that figuring things out often requires.

For instance, as the class progressed, we were more than happy to talk

---

9. Bryce Courtenay, *The Power of One* (New York: Ballantine, 1989), 106. In 1992 this book was made into a movie of the same title.

about God's use of marriage as a metaphor for Christ's relationship with the church. But what we really wanted to know was what we were supposed to do when the metaphor broke down because the husband went ballistic with the wife over how much money she spent on groceries last month. Or when the wife seriously wondered if she was really a Christian because she had a cold heart toward God for months after having their first child. Or when the topic of praying together (or more accurately, *not* praying together) became a burden to both the husband and the wife, but neither had a clue what to do about it. Megan and I weren't sure there were any easy answers for what we were wrestling with; all we wanted was to be allowed to ask some questions.

Working through issues (the process) takes energy, requires vulnerability and acceptance, and is a lot more work than most of us want to make time for. But this is the stuff life and learning are made of, and sometimes that means asking in-process questions rather than looking for the product of black-and-white answers.

Ready to Learn

Recently, an acquaintance approached me (Craig), looking for a job. He had been fired from his last two jobs and wondered if I might be able to help him out. We scheduled a time to meet, and he came over, dressed to the nines and obviously in interview mode. Forgoing the formalities and letting him know that I really didn't have anything for him, I asked him what had happened at his former job and how he was processing this recent series of events.

He admitted to causing some trouble for his supervisor but concluded that he was fired because their styles simply didn't gel. As I listened to him talk, I noticed that a lot of the problems he mentioned seemed to lie with him, but he had never asked for clarification or help in working through them. Instead, he viewed the whole situation as a battle between him and his supervisor that he eventually lost.

After he left I called his former supervisor and asked her for her version of the story, keeping my previous conversation confidential. I heard a totally different account from her, especially about the supposed styles discrepancy.

Apparently, the employee was unwilling to hear the supervisor's and others' feedback as to how his work could be more efficient. In a couple of cases, the employee made decisions that were inappropriate and even against direct instructions.

My acquaintance clearly went into the job thinking that he knew exactly what he was doing, and no one else could tell him otherwise. He was hired because he knew what he was doing in many ways; he was well qualified. He was fired because he didn't have an attitude of teachability that would help him grow.

Teachability means entering a situation prepared to learn. It means being interested in the people around you and in the stories they have to tell. A few years ago Julie and I (Doug) had a young couple over for dinner. We peppered them with questions throughout the evening with a genuine desire to learn more about them.[10] They, however, never once asked anything about us. While we didn't invite them over so we could talk about ourselves, it said a lot that they asked zero questions. The evening quickly passed with the hustle and bustle of eating and corralling our children. Still no questions. After we got the kids in bed, I finally said to them, "You should ask Julie how we met," which got them started and helped us learn from each other.

In encouraging this couple to talk to Julie, I was trying to point out that they needed to learn the art of asking questions. Why? Because we become more teachable when we initiate conversations with strangers, pastors, mentors, those we're mentoring, teachers, professors, coffee-shop regulars, cashiers, teenagers, old people…and the list goes on.

When my sister, Denise, was pregnant with her first child, Julie gave her one piece of advice: "Ask a lot of questions." Julie explained that she was so ignorant with our first child that many of her issues and problems would have been cleared up if only she had been more willing to ask "stupid" questions.

This advice speaks to all of us regardless of our childbearing status. Asking questions and learning from various situations and experiences help us to see how little we know and how many people we can learn from. We learn

---

10. I have learned about this from Julie as she is the greatest question asker I know.

when we take seriously the viewpoints of others, try to enter into what they are saying, and run it through the grid of God's Word. If we don't ask good questions, we'll be stunted in our learning and in our pursuit of understanding who we are.

Another good way to learn about our world and ourselves is to read books. We cannot make sense of the world around us and engage in the marketplace of ideas unless we read—new books, old books, familiar books, challenging books, fiction, nonfiction, religious books, and just plain good books.[11] Writer Anne Lamott says it well:

> For some of us, books are as important as almost anything else on Earth. What a miracle it is that out of these small, flat rigid squares of paper unfolds world after world, worlds that sing to you, comfort and quiet or excite you. Books help us understand how we are to behave. They show us what community and friendship mean; they show us how to live and idle. They are full of all the things that you don't get in real life—wonderful, lyrical language, for instance right off the bat. And quality of attention: we may notice amazing details during the course of a day but we rarely let ourselves stop and pay attention, and this is a great gift. My gratitude for good writing is unbounded; I'm grateful for it the way I'm grateful for the ocean. Aren't you?[12]

We also demonstrate our willingness to learn when we sometimes mull over crazy and scary ideas, not just study truth. "All great truths begin as blasphemies," said George Bernard Shaw. Sometimes we learn more about what's true when we learn about what's false. For instance, I (Craig) have never been that big of a Friedrich Nietzsche fan, largely because I had always heard that he said God was dead. This struck me as a more-than-slight doctrinal difference between him and me. But a few years ago, I decided to read some of what he wrote.

---

11. You can find some of our book recommendations in the back of this book.
12. Anne Lamott, *Bird by Bird* (New York: Knopf, 1994), 15.

I learned that Nietzsche actually scorned those who said "God is dead" but who continued living the same way as before. Nietzsche's point was that it's not possible to have Christian morality without Christian faith. "They are rid of the Christian God," he wrote in *Twilight of the Idols,* "and now believe all the more firmly that they must cling to the Christian morality.... When one gives up the Christian faith, one pulls the right to Christian morality out from under one's feet."[13]

Now Nietzsche won't find a place in many of our homes or church libraries and, well, that's fine. But the guy was right in some ways—we can't pretend to live "Christianly" if the Christian God for whom we are named seems dead to us. I had not really thought about that before, and surprisingly, I learned it from Nietzsche. What truths do we miss when we do not consider a few "lies" as well?

Another very practical way we learn is by doing what our moms said: Turn off the television, go outside to get some fresh air, and consider for a moment the beauty of the world.[14] Other ideas? Interview a grandparent and get his or her perspective on life. Quiet yourself and listen to God in prayer. Keep a journal. Learn to play a musical instrument, buy a telescope and take up astronomy, or watch a PBS special on the history of something instead of wasting an hour enduring *World's Scariest Car Crashes 27* on Fox. Or come up with your own list of ways to cultivate a sense of wonder so you won't have to read other people's lists in their books. Regardless, be intentional about noticing the opportunities around you to learn from others and their experiences.

Teachability Promotes Teachability

As if we needed a final reason to develop our teachability, here's one more for your consideration: Being teachable helps us teach others. Why is this? Two reasons: (1) Most people don't like to learn from arrogant teachers, and (2) we tend to share with others the things we've learned in our own lives.

13. Friedrich W. Nietzsche, *Twilight of the Idols,* in *The Portable Nietzsche,* ed. Walter Kaufmann (New York: Penguin, 1977), 515.
14. Read *Pilgrim at Tinker Creek* (New York: Harper, 1998) by Annie Dillard for some inspiration for getting out and "seeing" our world.

Ever been around people who preach the value of being teachable but don't seem to be teachable themselves? Chances are you won't be around them too long if you have a choice, because hypocrisy is a terrible teacher. This incongruence can be downright devastating in helping people grow personally and spiritually. When we try to instruct others about the need to be teachable without first modeling our own commitment to such a lifestyle, we end up teaching no one.

The Pharisees (or "separated ones") were notorious for hypocrisy. When they demonstrated that they were unwilling to be taught by Jesus, they became ineffectual in teaching others. Rather than modeling learners' hearts, they lectured heretical doctrine and legalism. Jesus asked the Pharisees, "Are you not in error because you do not know the Scriptures or the power of God?" (Mark 12:24). Jesus also alluded to the effect their deficiency had on others: "Woe to you experts in the law, because you have taken away the key to knowledge. You yourselves have not entered, and you have hindered those who were entering" (Luke 11:52).

The Pharisees did not realize they were doing this. If we had been there, we may have applauded them for their zeal to uphold what they thought were the teachings of the Bible. Though they misunderstood the law, they passionately defended it against all perceived attacks. But they missed the point.

John Fischer writes, "It is my firm belief that the prideful attitude of the Pharisees and the practice of measuring out righteousness are problems that affect not only Christians but everyone at some point. They are built into human nature.... Acceptance on the basis of performance was how most of us began our lives, and it's not easy to shake."[15]

The Pharisees couldn't hear the true teaching of Jesus regarding the law and everything else because they hadn't dealt with their own sin. The teachers needed to be taught. Although we may gain status and position, we must remember that we have to continue to learn from the Teacher or potentially suffer the fate of the Pharisees.

---

15. John Fischer, *12 Steps for the Recovering Pharisee (Like Me)* (Grand Rapids: Bethany, 2000), 10.

When our teachability increases, we become more attuned to the learning process of observing, interpreting, and applying, which makes us better teachers of this same process to others. If we ourselves are not curious and intentional about being taught, we shouldn't be frustrated when those we are helping aren't either. After all, they're not learning it from us!

Herman Melville once said, "We cannot live only for ourselves. A thousand fibers connect us with our fellow-men; and along those fibers, as sympathetic threads, our actions run as causes, and they come back to us as effects."

When God gave us life, he also gave each of us a story to tell—not just for our sakes but for the sakes of others. How well we tell our stories will depend on how much we learn from them ourselves.

A Sense of Wonder

Julie and I (Doug) recently took our kids to Florida. They had heard of the ocean, read about it, and seen it on television—but they'd never experienced it. The wonder and amazement on their faces could not have been any better for us to see: "It's so big! And loud! And look at the sand! Let's build sand castles and find shells and get wet!" They will never have a "first time" of seeing the ocean again. But we pray other "oceans" out there will captivate them the same way.

Seeing our kids' first ocean sighting reminded me of the first time *I* saw the ocean, and it reminded me that I have to be careful not to lose a sense of wonder. Can those crashing waves ever become commonplace in our lives? Can we forget how great it is to learn new things, see new places, meet new people? Many of us get so jaded in our experiences that we've forgotten how great it is to do something for the first time. Your first roller-coaster ride. Your first kiss. Your first job. Your first spring break. Your first child. Your first home. Your first car. Your first time to stay up past 3 A.M. Your first exposure to C. S. Lewis.

The more we cultivate an attitude of learning, the more we will be open to wonder, and the more firsts we will enjoy. This is one of the great privileges not just of our twenties but of our lives. When we make ourselves teachable, we make ourselves ready to be amazed, to be curious, to be changed.

Ideas of Things to Do

- Read the Bible, the greatest book of all. Read it looking for certain themes (sovereignty, love, grace, emotion, anger over sin). Read it looking for a better knowledge of the Father who loves you, the Savior who came and lived and died for you, and the Holy Spirit who lives in you. Look for the gospel in the Old Testament, which is all over the place.
- Look into taking a college course by extension or enrolling in a course or two at a local seminary or university. You don't have to get a degree, but the course material itself and the loving law of grades and tests might open you up to new ideas and greater knowledge of God.
- Read, read, read.
- Form a group that cares about theology and life, and take the time to study and talk over what you're learning.
- Invest in tapes of teachers who speak the truth in love.
- Review what you're learning and take inventory of the thoughts you already have.
- Apply your new knowledge to your life.

CHAPTER SIX

Faithfulness

THE CRUCIBLE OF THE TWENTIES

Faithfulness and sincerity are the highest things.
—CONFUCIUS

That we have but little faith is not sad, but that we have little faithfulness.
—HENRY DAVID THOREAU

L ike just about everyone else who has ever learned to sing or to play an instrument, I (Craig) have entertained the idea of doing "more" with music. Growing up, I dreamed of writing, recording, touring, and ministering, all in a two-year cycle as part of a lucrative contract I would sign. This, to me, was a great gig, and I hoped God would book it for me.

I started working toward this goal during high school. I knew I had to develop my stage presence and abilities, but in rural west central Illinois, well, let's just say there aren't exactly many venues for a sixteen-year-old keyboard player. In fact, I had to create my own. One summer I decided I would play nursing homes. After the accolades from those gigs began to pour in, I started playing more at church (my mom was the organist, so I had an "in"). There I performed "special music" (namely my own rock'n'roll versions of great Methodist hymns),[1] as well as musicals I wrote for my church youth group. I

---

1. I once rewrote the lyrics of "There Is a Balm in Gilead," changing the song to "There Is a Balm in Griggsville" (my hometown). I've written a lot of bad songs in my life, but this rewrite was easily one of the worst.

eventually formed a band, and we played a couple of local camps and youth functions. In my mind, it was only a matter of time before I hit it big.

Who knew there were other songwriters and musicians who had the same idea? Reality hit when I went to pitch songs in Nashville. I was trying to make something happen on a week-long trip—everyone else in Nashville was waiting tables, frequenting songwriting clubs, and using church as a place to make connections. I came home discouraged and confused. Why weren't the opportunities of the past five years leading anywhere now? What, God, had been the point of any of this?

In the wake of my Nashville experience, the Lord showed me the point by way of Luke 16:10: "Whoever can be trusted with very little can also be trusted with much, and whoever is dishonest with very little will also be dishonest with much." I began to understand that God was going to develop my faithfulness before he expanded my fruitfulness. Only then did I begin to realize that playing nursing homes and writing cutesy musicals and singing in a band for audiences numbering no more than ten people was not a waste of time but a way of training me to be faithful. I tried to be less concerned with the people who *didn't* show up and more concerned about those who did. Most important, I slowly came to understand that faithfulness is the key character quality of the twenties.

Faithful While We Wait

God uses us where we are, but he also continually develops us now for something to come later. Our childhood experiences become our adult expressions, our current job prepares us for a future career—and our humanity is preparation for eternity. The future "something else" may not always be bigger, better, or different than what we're doing now, or it could be all three. Who knows? The key for our future is to be faithful now in the midst of the lessons, relationships, experiences, tasks, and opportunities God brings about in our lives.

Consider Joseph, a fascinating twentysomething in the Scriptures. To paraphrase Genesis 37–50, here's a guy who grew up both wealthy and favored by his father, Jacob, but had weird dreams about how he would someday rule over his older brothers. Joseph made the mistake of telling his brothers this bit of information, which wasn't the smartest move he ever made. His dream telling got him sold into slavery, where he worked his way up to a prominent position in a government official's household only to be falsely accused of committing adultery with the government official's wife. Here we begin to see glimpses of Joseph's faithfulness. Although this official's wife had wanted the affair, Joseph remained faithful to his master and his God by refusing to enter into the dalliance with her.

The refusal itself unjustly got him thrown into prison. Yet again, when he had every opportunity to rage against the "machine," Joseph proved himself faithful. The Lord was with him, showing Joseph kindness and favor, and the jail warden promoted Joseph to a position of running prison operations. While working there, he had some strange conversations with a cupbearer and a baker before being pulled out of jail two years later (thanks to the cupbearer's tardy bit of networking) to interpret Pharaoh's bad dream. In interpreting that dream, Joseph formulated a plan to save the Egyptians from famine and death. This elevated him to second in command of the most powerful government in the world at the time. His new role placed him in a position to answer his brothers' pleas for help, fulfilling his childhood dreams as their ruler as well as reuniting him with his beloved father. The famine came, Joseph's plan worked, and they all lived happily ever after. (That is until one of Pharaoh's successors forgot about Joseph and enslaved Israel a couple of generations later, but, well, that's another story).

It's easy for us to remark at God's bizarre but constant leading of Joseph; in fact, we could not write Joseph's story any more strangely than God did himself. But consider what Joseph must have gone through personally in the midst of all the scenery change. Chances are he asked God why all this was happening, if he had done something wrong, and when any of his life would make sense. He probably whined some, reflected a lot, and prayed about what it was that was going on. He was a classic twentysomething: competent and willing, but scared about the future and uncertain about what God was doing or why.

As he was going through all of these experiences, Joseph probably never imagined that when he turned thirty he would be Pharaoh's chief of staff.

When he played cards with the cupbearer and the baker deep in the bowels of an Egyptian prison, he had no plan or guarantee that he would get out soon, no calendar with dates to cross off as he waited his way to freedom. For all Joseph knew, this was as good as it was going to get.

And yet it wasn't—freedom came. And as a result of his many different experiences in his twenties, Joseph developed a healthy understanding of himself and a strong reliance on God. His perspective on things is summed up in his own words to his brothers in Genesis 50:19-20: "Don't be afraid. Am I in the place of God? You intended to harm me, but God intended it for good to accomplish what is now being done, the saving of many lives." Through all the twists and turns of Joseph's life, he had ended up fulfilling God's purposes for him, the very things foretold in his dreams long ago. Joseph just hadn't been told *how* it would happen. Through all he encountered he was faithful, and God blessed him and his family as a result.

The Aroma of Sacrifice

In the book of Leviticus we frequently come across a phrase about burnt offerings: "an offering made by fire, an aroma pleasing to the Lord" (1:9,13,17, for example). To produce an "aroma pleasing to the Lord" required quite a fire to consume the sacrifice.

The Levitical sacrifices that the Israelites regularly observed were fulfilled in Christ's sacrifice. Yet in Romans we read that we are to be "living sacrifices" for God (12:1). If our lives are to be sacrificial ones with an "aroma pleasing to the Lord," we must be tried by fire. If you're anything like us, the idea of subjecting yourself to pain is not too motivating. But going through hurts is often part of what makes sacrifice sacrifice, and faithfulness faithfulness.

One of the most painful and agonizing tests I (Doug) ever experienced happened several years ago when Julie and I went to deliver our first baby. Julie had been bleeding and having contractions, which would have been okay except for the fact that all of this was happening three months too early.

She lay in the hospital in pain, and eventually the nurses drifted off until Julie sounded the warning cry: "I feel like I need to push! I need to push!" And there, in Stillwater, Oklahoma, Ruth—all of two pounds, five ounces, small enough to fit in a tiny shoebox—came into the world. They whisked her away, did a few tests, and finally told us that we had a little girl who was making it, but they were going to airlift her to Tulsa for more specialized care. They then wheeled her into our room in her plastic ventilator for five minutes before taking her away again.

We cleaned up and drove to Tulsa to begin the routine that would be our lives for the next three months: washing up to prevent infection, feeding Ruth, watching her grow and gain strength, seeing other babies go in for surgery and wondering if that would be our daughter one day. Our baby was in a hospital fighting for her life, and we couldn't do anything for her. Julie was physically and mentally exhausted and yet somehow strong on the inside. I, on the other hand, put up a good front but was barely coping on the inside. Months later the hospital sent Ruth home with a monitor strapped around her chest to make sure she didn't stop breathing for more than fifteen seconds.[2] That was hell—and almost too much for me.

Sometimes I wanted to fly to Argentina—or anywhere!—never to return, because I thought I couldn't handle the responsibility. I considered running away from my problems, leaving a single mother behind, and marrying someone else who wouldn't be such a burden. (These are thoughts I wasn't honest about until years later.) By God's grace, I got through that time and, thankfully, so did Ruth. She is now nine, healthy, and engrossed in writing, drawing, and reading. Our faith helped; our friends, family, and church helped. It's a good thing we had that support because my faithfulness—to Ruth, to Julie, to God—was tested in a big way during that time.

Next Stop: Struggleville

As you probably already know if you're in your twenties, life isn't going to be all vanilla lattes. You might lose a child or suffer at the hands of an unloving

---

2. That machine beeped like the McDonald's French-fry machine warning that the fries are going to burn soon. That sound is forever etched in my memory.

spouse. You might flip out as a result of nagging, manipulative parents or get physically sick and lose hope for a while. You might get laid off from your job and wonder if this is the beginning of the end. Change can seem to come at warp speed or so slowly that you wonder if you'll be able to endure the wait.

In addition, it's impossible to prepare completely for whatever pain may come because you don't know what form it will take. It will come, though; it's not *if*, it's *when*. In the eloquent words of Bill Mallonee, lead singer of the band *Vigilantes of Love,* "Welcome all you suckers to Struggleville."[3]

A mutual friend of ours recently pulled into "Struggleville" when everything he had worked for was almost stripped away. Twenty-eight years old, with a master's in accounting, Trevor had been working for months to begin his own business with his personal savings. All was going well until he didn't receive the loan he had expected, and within a few weeks he was staring at a lawsuit from those who had expected to be employed by him as well as the prospect of jail time for defaulted checks. As Trevor and I (Doug) sat across from each other, I could see the despair in his eyes as he explained his situation and told me about his new job as a cashier at Target.

If we answer the who-am-I question with things like status, money, promotion, power, or feelings, then when any of those things falls apart, we are shaken—we don't have much solid ground to stand on anymore. Likewise, when the dreams, aspirations, and relationships we have held dear are taken from us, we are forced to look at what we've been trusting in.[4] It's particularly in tough times like these that we need to be faithful. This means trusting in God, claiming his promises, honestly assessing our situation, and clinging to what we know to be true. Faithfulness despite our frustrations means that we offer our lives wholly and completely to God instead of blaming him for our plight.

My (Craig's) wife, Megan, attends a Bible study with an older woman named Darnly, whose husband was in a car crash years ago, was hospitalized for nearly five months, and was never mentally the same afterward. Although

---

3. Bill Mallonee, "Welcome to Struggleville," 1994. *Welcome to Struggleville,* Capricorn.
4. Sheldon Vanauken's *A Severe Mercy* (San Francisco: HarperSanFrancisco, 2003) will rock your world on this score. His amazing wife died, and he finally had to admit that it was the best thing that could have happened to either of them. You will cry.

he's physically intact, Larry can't be left alone and needs assistance going to the bathroom. He is essentially Darnly's fourth child but with no chance of ever growing up.

"For months I believed with all my heart that God would heal Larry," says Darnly, "but then the day came when I realized that Larry would probably never be Larry again—never hold me in his arms as a husband does, never be a real father to his children, never be able to hold a logical conversation when he could help make a decision. My world crashed and I wanted to run as far away as I could.

"The key," she continues, "to being able to live in circumstances that were not my dream of marriage—circumstances that did not make me happy or fulfill my needs—was threefold: I learned I had to be content with Larry just as he was, I had to focus on my responsibilities and not think about my 'rights' in the situation, and I had to learn to let God be God and use my life to draw others to himself. My responsibility as Larry's wife was to do the very best I could for him, because that is what love is all about." And this, by the grace of God, is what Darnly has done for the past twenty-seven years.[5]

In 2 Corinthians 1:8-9, Paul wrote:

> We do not want you to be uninformed, brothers, about the hardships
> we suffered in the province of Asia. We were under great pressure, far
> beyond our ability to endure, so that we despaired even of life. Indeed,
> in our hearts we felt the sentence of death. But this happened that we
> might not rely on ourselves but on God, who raises the dead.

Paul's words help us remember that suffering has a greater purpose—to strip away all the things in which we put our significance and trust and to allow us to see our oft-forgotten frailty and our need to rely on God for all we are lacking.

---

5. The brain damage Larry suffered causes him to say some things over and over again in response to certain statements. One of the things Larry says often is "God is in charge!" According to Darnly, learning to accept that in her life has been a good thing and exactly what God wanted for them as a couple. Now that's a perspective of faithfulness.

If we had been around Paul, we would have seen that he wasn't chipper all the time—after all, he says he "despaired even of life," which sounds pretty intense. Yet we know he got through it and was able to give this testimony: "This happened that we might not rely on ourselves but on God." Like Joseph, Paul had come to believe that "Struggleville" happened so that he could know God and himself in a deeper way than he did before.

Faithful in the Small Stuff

It's not just in the big situations that God expects us to be faithful. We are to be faithful in the smallest of things as well. In his book *12 Steps for the Recovering Pharisee (Like Me),* musician and author John Fischer writes:

> When God calls for perfection, it is assumed I cannot perform it. It's the demand for perfection that keeps me relying on God's mercy and grace. But the call to faithfulness is a call I can answer. Faithful to follow, faithful to confess, faithful to obey, faithful to repent, faithful to believe, faithful to pray and seek God—all these are requirements of faithfulness.[6]

One summer I (Doug) worked at a pool store and carried five-gallon jugs of chlorine around all day. The die-cast plastic handles tore into my hands, my hair bleached white, and my shoes were eaten alive by the toxins. It was the worst job I've ever had because it felt so meaningless. God really worked on my character that summer, partly through that job at Missouri Pool. I spent megatime—just God and me—talking, singing, wondering, lamenting. He taught me how to work hard and with integrity as I slugged away as the resident grunt boy.

The Barenaked Ladies (a band that has no actual unclad women in it) has a song called *Never Is Enough* in which they sing about how happy they are

---

6. John Fischer, *12 Steps for the Recovering Pharisee (Like Me)* (Grand Rapids: Bethany, 2000), 21.

that they didn't have to do the menial tasks of youth, and now they get to do whatever they want. They didn't have to work at the mall or at Wendy's. They didn't have to shear Christmas trees for a whole summer as Craig once did. But the thing is that those kinds of chores can be tremendous growth opportunities for us if we remember that God is working on our character in the midst of them.

Remember Craig's friend and mentor, Jack? Jack tells the story of his job as an assistant to Lorne Sanny. One of Jack's tasks in that position was to clean the Sannys' bathrooms. One day, when he was trying to get the job done in a hurry, Jack called Lorne's wife, Lucy, in for a final inspection, upon which she promptly checked behind the toilet, knowing if he cleaned there, everywhere else would be clean as well. He hadn't. Lucy's words: "If you've not been faithful with someone else's property, what makes you think God will give you property of your own?" That experience marked him so much that he and Shaunda always made an effort to leave every apartment they rented better than they found it, in hopes that one day God would entrust them with a home of their own—which they now have.

Even the hardest jobs are redeemable. We shouldn't avoid them or ignore their benefits just because they're hard. This may mean starting as an intern at a company even though you wanted to enter at a higher position. It may mean putting a career on hold to care for an unexpected baby even though you weren't planning to be a parent for several years. It may mean figuring out how to make the most of a long commute to a job because you need to stay at the job long enough to save up money for graduate school. Being faithful in these kinds of difficult situations doesn't mean allowing yourself to be walked on "for the sake of the kingdom." It also doesn't mean that you shouldn't aspire to a different position someday. But you *can* look for what God is doing right where you are and be faithful to make the best of a situation that doesn't seem "successful" at the time.

Despite what our culture says, it's good to work above and beyond the reward of a paycheck, to labor and create without "adequate" equal-to-the-product recompense, to serve people because you want to serve them, not just because you want to get ahead. This is how we learn to work hard and well.

This may mean that you won't be in the most fulfilling job you'll ever have, but your perspective if and when you get that fulfilling job will be different because of the path you traveled earlier.

Jesus told the story of a man who was given money from his master and then doubled that investment. "Well done, good and faithful servant!" the master told the servant. "You have been faithful with a few things; I will put you in charge of many things. Come and share your master's happiness" (Matthew 25:21). The master was also happy with the man who doubled an investment of lesser value. The master was extremely unhappy, though, with the man who buried his money and returned only the amount he had received.

The issue wasn't the amount of the return, but the faithfulness and attitude of the servant. The men who invested the money understood that the master loved them and wanted them to share in his happiness. They did a good job with the amount they were given, and their understanding of the master's expectations led to fruitfulness and praise. The other man told the master, "I knew that you are a hard man, harvesting where you have not sown and gathering where you have not scattered seed. So I was afraid and went out and hid your talent in the ground" (Matthew 25:24-25). This servant didn't understand the master, trying to make excuses and slander his master's character. This led to disobedience and shame.

What does this mean for us? It means that God calls us to do our best with whatever we've been given. We should take every opportunity, however small, and do what we can to bring about goodness in that job. The reason and result are interconnected. Because we know that God is good and desires the best for us, we know that every opportunity he puts before us is for our good. When we do our best to please him, we receive praise for our faithfulness, and we know his goodness even more deeply as we enter into his happiness.

As we develop faithfulness in our twenties, God will reward us with more opportunities in our families, our churches, and our professions. Because of the lessons learned cleaning bathrooms, changing diapers, making copies, and working late, we will be able to serve effectively in areas that are less "earthy" than the others. When we are asked to do a task, no matter how high or low on the job totem pole it ranks, we should remember the words of the master who invited the servants into the master's happiness: "Well done, good and faithful servant!"

Reputation or Relationship?

Proverbs 21:27 says, "The sacrifice of the wicked is detestable—how much more so when brought with evil intent!" Sometimes we may want to make sacrifices only to look good to those around us, but God calls us to be faithful for the right reasons, not just because it makes us feel good when we compare ourselves to others.

I (Craig) don't think I've ever had a pure motive in my life. A lot of my early attempts at what appeared to be faithfulness came out of not ever wanting to drop the ball in anything I was asked to do. I wanted to appear diligent and hoped to be praised for my efforts; my reputation as a competent believer—not necessarily my relationship with Christ—became a major reason for faithfulness.

As a result, I became known for my skill in rarely missing a detail, but I developed a severe case of legalism in the process, holding others and myself to standards beyond what even the Lord required. My legalistic tendencies were a *reaction* to my desire to prove my faithfulness rather than a *response* to the God who loves me and asks me to be faithful because he is faithful to me. Even now, when I am asked to do something, I have to be very careful not to make the mistake of showing others what I can *do*. I must remember to do the task well because of who I *am*—one called to be faithful by the One who is faithful.

In Psalm 51 we read David's prayer of repentance resulting from the Bathsheba debacle. He said, "You do not delight in sacrifice, or I would bring it; you do not take pleasure in burnt offerings" (verse 16). If we're familiar with the rest of the Old Testament, that statement seems off. God is commanding sacrifices all the time. Why did David say this? He continued: "The sacrifices of God are a broken spirit; a broken and contrite heart, O God, you will not despise" (verse 17). David realized that his sacrifices didn't automatically deal with his inner issues. They pictured these issues for him, but until he saw his relationship with God restored, he could sacrifice a million animals to no avail.

Our actions and our hearts need to go together. We must monitor our motives, but we should also not sit around waiting until we feel like our reasons are all right and pure. They're intertwined. Sometimes the action might lead to the motive or vice versa, but both should coalesce into a final place—a relationship of faithfulness with Christ.

In our twenties we must focus not on what we are seen doing for the Lord as a motivation to be faithful but rather on making sure that what we do naturally flows out of the relationship we are cultivating with him. This helps us guard against creating our own appearances of sacrificial obedience or die-on-the-hill martyrdom and instead enables us to simply obey what God has commanded us to do, which is really all faithfulness is.

The Glue That Holds It All Together

We said in chapter 1 that it's good to experiment, ask questions, and explore in our twenties. That doesn't mean that it's a great idea to bounce around between cities, jobs, friends, and churches. While it's true that in our twenties we need to be malleable, not too quick to assume that our job, our marital status, or the city we live in defines us, we also have to have balance or we will flake out and never make commitments.

In reality we discover who we are by making and being faithful to our commitments. For instance, no one is every really *ready* to get married, but you can't wait until you're "ready" to take that step. You become ready by becoming married, and the commitment you make that day begins the lifelong process of figuring out who you are as a husband or wife. Our faithfulness in the midst of our commitments shapes the development of all the other character traits we've discussed and helps bring our true identity into view.

For example, our faithfulness to pursue the right understanding of ourselves and of God shows that we are learning humility. When we start to see what we are lacking—and how much we need Christ—it takes perseverance to keep our commitment to know God. Faithfulness tells us to keep going in thinking rightly about ourselves—not too highly, but not too pitifully either.

Faithfulness also strengthens our integrity. You may be tempted to bow out of a lease too early, to pretend not to hear a comment, to tell a white lie here or there, or to put on a facade instead of being yourself. Faithfulness says that you live honestly, that again and again you go to your friends, family, church, and community to hear the truth, to repent of your sins, and to be called once more to the gospel of grace.

Our faithfulness to stick with our church and our friends reveals our teachability. Many times we're tempted to bail out of one of our commitments when they get hard or when they reveal to us that we're not exactly who we want to be. But our faithfulness demonstrates that we understand God has put these opportunities in our lives to help us know ourselves and him better.

Many of us run the risk of never developing in these areas because we skip around from place to place, avoiding the contexts in which faithfulness can be developed. Sometimes that can't be helped; sometimes God calls us to intentionally and prayerfully look for something new. But when we land geographically or relationally, our desire should be to invest in that place. We can't always be *going* somewhere. We need to *be where we are*—one hundred percent—growing in humility, integrity, teachability, and faithfulness.

Ideas of Things to Do

- Look for chances to serve others in little ways.
- Read books and biographies about people who overcame incredibly difficult circumstances and were faithful in the process. There's nothing like life-examples to motivate us.
- Do a good job in every little task you're given, especially the ones nobody else wants.
- Pursue excellence without driving everyone else crazy. In other words, know when to draw the line between excellence and "control freak."
- Check your motives, preferably with someone who will be honest enough to call you on impure ones (spouses are particularly good for this).

- Make commitments and do everything physically possible to keep them.
- Guard your integrity and faithfulness like a bulldog: Do what you say you will. Apologize when you don't. Don't slander, but tell the truth. These are little decisions that crop up all the time that put legs to our faithfulness.

We should be careful to get out of an experience only the wisdom that is in it—and stop there; lest we be like the cat that sits down on a hot stove-lid. She will never sit down on a hot stove-lid again—and that is well; but also she will never sit down on a cold one anymore.

—MARK TWAIN, Pudd'nhead Wilson's new calendar

As human beings, we all make meaning. We search for a sense of connection, pattern, order, and significance. In our ongoing interaction with all of life, we puzzle about the fitting, truthful relationships among things. We search for ways of understanding our experience that make sense of both the expected and the unexpected in everyday life.

—SHARON DALOZ PARKS, *Big Questions, Worthy Dreams*

Worldview

Many of us work hard to segment our lives into various compartments—faith, family, politics, work, holiday. We do this because we are told to by our culture and because that way of thinking allows us to keep on trucking in each area without considering how these spheres might influence one another. Church on Sundays. Family at home. Who we voted for in the ballot box. Work stays work. The lake on the weekends. We try to motor along without bringing them all together.

But at some point in our twenties, we start to ask more questions: What is the nature of the world? What is the meaning of human history? Am I lovable? What are the values and limitations of my culture? Do I want to get married? Why? What is the meaning of money? What constitutes meaningful work? What do I want the future to look like?[1]

Our answers to those big questions reveal our beliefs about ourselves, our God, and our lives. We begin to see that our questions, our answers, our beliefs, and our actions are interwoven. We begin to examine our worldview.[2]

Our worldview is the way we look at things. It is the lens through which we see, the grid through which we evaluate life, and the matrix we've accepted as the way things work. We've formed these ideas about life in various ways as we've grown up. We've made observations through our experiences. We've accepted values and beliefs passed down from our parents and our society. We've processed concepts we call religion. We've trusted things as true and rejected others as false. Throughout our lives, we confirm that our worldview is accurate, or we bump into a situation in which our worldview isn't working quite right, and we tweak our outlook a bit.

All this usually happens without much fanfare as we're growing up, but in our twenties we begin to take a look at the matrix itself and examine whether there may be some fatal flaws in the system. We also start to look at where exactly we acquired the grid through which we process life. When someone

---

1. Questions taken from Sharon Daloz Parks, *Big Questions, Worthy Dreams: Mentoring Young Adults in Their Search for Meaning, Purpose, and Faith* (San Francisco: Jossey-Bass, 2000), 137-8.
2. Adapted from Steven Garber, *The Fabric of Faithfulness* (Downer's Grove, Ill.: Inter-Varsity, 1997), 16.

does this, for example, she may find that because her father did not give her the kind of love she craved, she's formed a worldview that says men aren't faithful and can't express love. Now when she meets a man, she unconsciously puts him up against that grid and evaluates whether he confirms or confuses that worldview. The same is true for anything—politics, food, God, bicycles, rhubarb, whatever.

At Christmas we sing "Joy to the World" and proclaim that Jesus the King will bring his kingdom "far as the curse is found." How far is that? Every place sin has touched, which is *everywhere*. All our various boxes can be touched by the transforming gospel of Jesus because he is the King of all the world. As we begin to understand our worldview better, we see that the lordship of Christ matters in every area of our lives. And yet it takes time to figure out why we think what we think and then to line up those ideas with the Scriptures. Our twenties are the perfect time to hash out some of these ideas by ourselves and with one another. Here we can begin to live authentically in every area of our lives.

You may be farther along in processing many of these thoughts—or maybe not. Your worldview may be driving decisions in ways you don't even realize. The next five chapters deal with a few of the worldview issues we encounter most distinctively—money, time, relationships, community, and legacy. There could be a thousand more chapters because, as we've mentioned, worldview issues touch on every area of life, but we've chosen these because they seem particularly relevant to our twenties.

Let the discussion continue.

CHAPTER SEVEN

Money

RESISTING THE AMERICAN DREAM

We have become too self-sufficient to feel the necessity
of redeeming and preserving grace.

—ABRAHAM LINCOLN, National Feast Day proclamation in 1863

The greatest enemy of hunger for God is not poison but apple pie.
It is not the banquet of the wicked that dulls our appetite for heaven,
but endless nibbling at the table of the world...the greatest adversary
of love to God is not his enemies but his gifts. And the most deadly
appetites are not for the poison of evil, but for the simple pleasures
of Earth. For when these replace an appetite for God Himself,
the idolatry is scarcely recognizable, and almost incurable.

—JOHN PIPER, *A Hunger for God*

Maybe your version of the American Dream is a bit like mine (Doug's). I think of a cool house with a garage filled with tools (okay, so this is the male version of the dream) and a place upstairs where I can read by the fire and relax with my latest version of Nintendo. My kids are happy and well adjusted. They love me and get to fulfill their interests in music, soccer, science, or whatever will eventually get them into a top-notch college. They're driven around town either by my always beautiful, loving, and responsive wife in a safe-yet-sporty minivan or by me in my monster SUV.[1] On the weekends

---

1. Gas prices stay amazingly low in my version of the American Dream.

I go for country drives on my Harley to our cabin, and in the summers (every summer, mind you) we take vacations to exotic places around the globe.

Sound familiar? You may want to add more shoes, exquisite food, or season tickets to Cardinals games to your dream. And some of you may have achieved a few of these things already. But will any of this truly make us happy? Will these things congeal into a ball of contentment and satisfaction, or will we end up seeing one day that we gave ourselves to the wrong goals—that we dreamed the wrong dream to begin with?[2]

If we stop to think about it, we realize that affluence has replaced God as the object of faith for many in America. We worship abundance, aspire to wealth, and continually mumble, "We deserve better." The truth is, we are a wasteful, extravagant bunch.[3] By whose standards do we deserve better? Let's face it: We live well, and frankly, we think we're supposed to.

We have such faith in our culture of consumption that, if we're not careful, we'll spend our lives accumulating things we'll never need. America has created an entire storage industry, in fact, because of our abundance of stuff. Fifty years ago, a fifteen-hundred-square-foot house was enough to raise a family of four; today, fifteen hundred square feet is barely the size of some basements. Families with two-car garages park neither of their vehicles in them because they need the space to store their extra belongings. Our economy, which used to be evaluated by how much we could produce, is now evaluated by how much we can consume. But how many cars, houses, and computers do we really need? When do we ever have enough?

A friend of ours, Leslie, is on the other side of the American Dream. She has all the "enough" she once wanted—and yet she still finds happiness elusive: "My dream was to marry a guy with a great job, have a few kids, and get

---

2. This was what the movie *American Beauty* was all about. We can't exactly recommend it since it has nudity, sex scenes, and violence in it, but the basic theme was that a house in the suburbs and a nice, cushy job can lead to completely messed-up lives instead of a picture-book existence.
3. For example, the United States has approximately 16 percent of the world's population but uses approximately 80 percent of its energy.

to stay home. All I wanted the first few years we were married was to get started on the family. Randy and I both had good jobs, were playing, making friends, whatever, and still, all I could think about was when my real life would start.

"Eventually, we had two boys. I got the stay-at-home part, but no money for cable or baby-sitters. I had a good sense that that time was temporary. 'Enjoy it now, because they won't be little long,' others told me. But I would still be looking ahead to when our sons would be bigger. Always looking ahead.

"Now, the boys are at a great age (nine and eleven), and Randy's job has taken off, so I have the golden-husband part. We are fortunate to be able to have two mortgages, three cars, and an old boat, and we can pay the hundreds of dollars a month in insurance that all our stuff requires—oh, plus we have an extra policy to cover us in case our other policies aren't enough. And we have cable.

"So my American Dream has come true, and I am happy—but I wouldn't say fulfilled. I order catalogs from graduate schools, look at the help-wanted ads, and volunteer thirty hours a week. This all makes me think I'm still look- ing for something. And I do wonder, *What was my hurry?*"

Though few of us can relate to Leslie's degree of materialistic success, all of us can feel some of her pathos expressed in her thoughts: *What does it take to be fulfilled? Why do I keep pursuing the dream, even when I know accumulat- ing stuff isn't what life is about?*

Our purpose in this chapter isn't to show the disparity between the haves and the have-nots or to become prognosticators, predicting gloom and doom, inflation and Wall Street meltdowns. What we want to do is point out that as Christians in our twenties, we are called to bring everything under the lord- ship of Jesus Christ. That includes our spending habits, our view of money and its worth, and our ideas about owning and taking care of whatever pieces of the world God may entrust to us. Deconstructing and then rebuilding our worldview on this issue and making new choices in light of our new under- standing helps us to be better stewards instead of richer slaves. As they say in the commercials: Priceless.

Adulterating Ourselves

In the book of Hosea, we read of how God commanded Hosea to marry a prostitute, Gomer. God knew (and actually told Hosea) that Gomer would betray Hosea, yet God still instructed him to marry her, which Hosea did out of obedience. They had a couple of kids, and then, sure enough, she started shacking up with another guy, leaving Hosea and the family. But in Hosea 3:1, "The LORD said to me [Hosea], 'Go, show your love to your wife again, though she is loved by another and is an adulteress. Love her as the LORD loves the Israelites, though they turn to other gods and love the sacred raisin cakes." So Hosea bought Gomer out of prostitution (his own wife, mind you!) and made another covenant with her, despite their past troubles.

The book of Hosea offers an illustration of God's redeeming love for an adulterous Israel. The story can also parallel our corporate and individual relationships with God. We are Gomer. Just as Gomer was "loved by another and is an adulteress," so we offer our affections to other things when they should be offered only to God.

In Hosea 3:4, God says that Israel "will live many days without king or prince, without sacrifice or sacred stones, without ephod or idol." God says he will strip away from the Israelites the things they have been trusting in—leaders, false gods, superstitions—instead of him. He does this so that "afterward the Israelites will return and seek the LORD their God and David their king. They will come trembling to the LORD and to his blessings in the last days" (verse 5).

God cared enough about the Israelites that he granted their desire to return to him in repentance. He then illustrated this redemption in a very real way—Hosea bought back his wife, someone who was already supposed to have been his—and restored his blemished bride to himself.

As God's people today we, too, are being called to return to him, to no longer be taken by the love of the world. We are to turn away from the earthly places we go to find love, satisfaction, and significance and come back to our bridegroom, Christ. The Hosea story is not about money, but the application to money is natural: We run to money and possessions because they give us status and position in our culture.

Money isn't the only god we lust after. But it's true that "the love of money is a root of all kinds of evil" (1 Timothy 6:10), and our desire for wealth is often the catalyst for our distance from God. We look at the parking lot and size up who has made it and who hasn't. We establish a continuum of importance based on our office location, the neighborhood we live in, even the amount of memory on our computers. In our minds, more is better, and we want to be the ones with more.

Even the church isn't immune to the quest for the accumulation of wealth. We shouldn't be too surprised at this because the church is made up of sinful people—us—who need Jesus to change our ideas and views about a lot of things, including money. Many of our churches want a bigger building to heighten their presence in the community, a larger budget to show growth, another pastor to extend their reach...for all the wrong reasons.[4] Although the church needs money to operate, it can begin to trust in the money itself and not in the One who gives the money in the first place.

Jesus warned, "Where your treasure is, there your heart will be also" (Matthew 6:21). Our treasure often lies in our buildings and in our things, in our programs and in our marketing, in our houses and in our stuff. Material resources no longer become the means to an end; they become the end in themselves.

It's a tough but real assessment, one that takes courage for the church and for us as individuals to own. Tom Sine puts it this way in his book *Mustard Seed versus McWorld*:

> My generation sold this generation the wrong dream. For all the talk
> about the lordship of Jesus, my generation sold the young the Ameri-
> can Dream with a little Jesus overlay. For all the talk about lordship,

---

4. It's important to note that there are thousands of churches of a variety of sizes that don't think this way. But the temptation is always there.

the real message to the Christian young is the message that drives McWorld. Agenda one is getting ahead in your job, getting ahead in the suburbs, getting your upscale lifestyle started; then, with whatever you have left, follow Jesus.[5]

Sine goes on to say that, "As we have seen, if the new generation puts the American Dream first, they will have little time or money to invest in the mission of the mustard seed."[6]

Without a redeemed understanding of money, our materialistic culture will woo us away from Christ. Yet God loves us enough to call us back to himself, away from the lies that surround us. Responding to that call can be a struggle, but the rewards are great. We are investing in the only mission that will last; we are investing in the kingdom of God here on earth.

Dreaming the Biblical Dream

The world tells us that the American Dream will give us fulfillment and success. We'd like to suggest that the Biblical Dream promises and delivers *significance*. But first we need to change our idea of what significance really is.

Look at the Beatitudes in Matthew 5. Blessed are those who mourn? Blessed are those who are persecuted? We usually think these things will bring about our ruin, not our happiness.[7] We run from pain rather than embrace it. We seek to be liked at any cost, not persecuted for our beliefs or actions. And we want to be comfortable financially and otherwise in the process.

But Jesus says something different in this passage. Even if we understand intellectually that he must be telling us how we should live, our hearts have trouble grasping that fact. C. S. Lewis said it this way: "Prosperity knits a man

---

5. Tom Sine, *Mustard Seed versus McWorld* (Grand Rapids: Baker, 1999), 137.
6. Sine, *Mustard Seed,* 137.
7. Youth worker and all-around general nut case for Christ Mike Yaconelli writes, "Ministry based on the Jesus of the Bible is disruptive, threatening, risky, dangerous, frightening, unstable, and unpredictable" ("The Power of One," *Youthworker Journal,* March/April 1998.)

to the world. He feels that he is finding his place in it, while really it is finding its place in him."[8] When the world numbs us to truth, it can be easy to hear or read something challenging—something life-altering—and walk away unchanged.

We might be startled at times at how skewed our worldview has become. I (Craig) once came across an article in *Newsweek* on graduating high-school seniors. As a college graduate, it depressed me to read that I made about as much as a male *without* a high-school degree. Someone could have preached a whole sermon to me about "counting the cost," "giving one's life to people," and "sacrifice," but I wasn't in the mood to hear it at the time. I felt like a fool for laboring for so little gain. While the vision for my ministry was still strong in me, I wondered if I could overcome the temptation of seeking a higher-salary job in an attempt to have a higher profile of myself.

Our society places so much emphasis on having the latest gadget or the absolute best quality that we've forgotten what the Bible says about success. In Joshua 1:7-8, Joshua told the Israelites,

> Be strong and very courageous. Be careful to obey all the law my servant
> Moses gave you; do not turn from it to the right or to the left, that you
> may be successful wherever you go. Do not let this Book of the Law
> depart from your mouth; meditate on it day and night, so that you may
> be careful to do everything written in it. Then you will be prosperous
> and successful.

God wanted Israel to be prosperous and successful. Isn't that what we want as well? But Joshua told the Israelites not to define success in the worldly way. Success would not be found in the amount of gold or sheep they owned or in the number of cities they conquered but in following the way of the Lord. Similarly, success today is not tied to bank accounts or designer clothes or corporate takeovers but in continuing faithfully in the path God has given us. We appreciate how the authors of *Repacking Your*

---

8. C. S. Lewis, *The Screwtape Letters* (Uhrichsville, Ohio: Barbour, 1990), 143.

Bags have attempted to break down the American Dream and promote a more biblical one. They define "the good life" as "living in the place you belong, with the people you love, doing the right work, on purpose."[9] That seems like a great start; it challenges us to take stock of where all those things are in our lives.

If we, in our twenties, can figure out the differences between the American Dream and the Biblical Dream, we can begin to think critically about the decisions that will come our way—where to live or what car to buy or what kind of job to take. Sometimes our decisions will seem countercultural to those around us. We may resist the idea of going into huge debt on a house even though that's what everyone else is doing. We may think twice about getting that second car just because it's more convenient than catching the bus. We may realize that we don't really *need* all the latest appliances that are advertised, even though others seem to think we do.

The point is, we don't have to be in junior high again to experience peer pressure; we can be full-fledged adults and never get away from the expectations placed on us by our friends, families, and culture. But God calls us to be defined by him, not by the things the world says are important. If our faith does not demand decisions that are at times in contrast to the world's, what kind of faith do we really have?

The Key to Our Dilemma

After thinking about all this, you may be tempted to swing to the other extreme, assuming that if rampant consumption is wrong, we should own only one change of clothing and forsake all worldly possessions. Is it wrong to own stuff? Is it wrong to want things?

The answer to that is a resounding NO. It's not wrong to own or want stuff. God created the earth and gave everything in it to us to take care of. A desire to have stuff is part of who we are. In fact, one of the most dehuman-

---

9. Richard J. Leider and David A. Shapiro, *Repacking Your Bags* (San Francisco: Berrett-Koehler, 1995), 26.

izing things to do to people is to take everything away so they have nothing. We need things to take care of. It's part of what makes us human.

And that's good. In Deuteronomy 8, when God took the Israelites out of slavery and gave them the Promised Land and all that was in it, he said:

For the LORD your God is bringing you into a good land—a land with streams and pools of water, with springs flowing in the valleys and hills, a land with wheat and barley, vines and fig trees, pomegranates, olive oil and honey; a land where bread will not be scarce and you will lack nothing; a land where rocks are iron and you can dig copper out of the hills.

When you have eaten and are satisfied, praise the LORD your God for the good land he has given you. (verses 7-10)

Look at all the things God gave to his people. He didn't intend for them to enter the Promised Land and sit around and do nothing all day. He meant for them to work and fulfill their callings and enjoy everything he gave them. Commentator J. A. Thompson writes, "Clearly it was God's intention that His people should enjoy His good gifts. It is no part of biblical faith to espouse a view of life that bans enjoyment and pleasure. It is, indeed, a misunderstanding of the facts of the case, that those who live according to God's laws are unhappy people."[10]

So we are set free to own things. To take care of them and use them to make our lives and the lives around us better. But these things are not to *define* us. We should use them, appreciate them, and offer them up to the Lord.

Paul's words in Philippians 4:12-13 give us some insight into how we should view our world and our place in it:

I know what it is to be in need, and I know what it is to have plenty. I have learned the secret of being content in any and every situation,

---

10. J. A. Thompson, *Deuteronomy: An Introduction and Commentary* (Downer's Grove, Ill.: InterVarsity, 1974), 136.

whether well fed or hungry, whether living in plenty or in want. I can do everything through him who gives me strength.

Contentment—not greed or asceticism—is the key to figuring out this tension between the American Dream and the Biblical Dream. We can have or not have this house—it shouldn't crush us if we don't get it or wholly fulfill us if we do. We can appreciate our car and not constantly scan the ads for a better one. We can earn a living, even a good one. We can desire to make as much money as we can—if we keep a broader and biblical perspective in mind.

It's tough to maintain the proper tension: Make as much as you can *and* be content with what you have. But that is our biblical calling. Money isn't evil, but "the *love* of money is a root of all kinds of evil" (1 Timothy 6:10). That's a big difference.

Late singer/songwriter Rich Mullins faced this same struggle:

Beaker [his roommate and fellow band member] and I started looking at three traditional monastic vows the Franciscans all take: the vow of poverty, the vow of obedience, and the vow of chastity. And we started saying, "What does that look like if you're not a monk?" We began to look at them in a broader sense rather than very specifically. We came to believe that poverty is being a steward of whatever resources you have, as opposed to being the owner of those resources, that what is important is to recognize that everything belongs to God, and He allows us to be stewards of His gifts. And so, rather than saying, "Okay, so we will just not own anything," we tried to look at everything that we own—our talents, our physical possessions—as being God's, and ourselves as being stewards of them.[11]

If we view our closets, our garages, and our refrigerators with the eyes of stewardship, we may begin to see things a bit differently. Recently I (Doug)

11. Rich Mullins, radio interview by Bob Michaels, Light 99, KTLI, Wichita, Kansas, for the premiere of *Canticle of the Plains,* 2 February 1997.

was shocked to realize how many dress shirts, pants, and shoes I have. Our culture of consumerism gets us to believe we need to buy clothes as if we're hoarding them for a cotton crisis. When I pass Old Navy, I want to see their sales just in case they have a cool long-sleeved oxford on the sale rack for only $9.99. Do I *need* another one? No way, but hey, I could always *use* another one, right?

Not only do we need less stuff, we need to be content with what we have. There will always be those who have more or less than we do. But when we learn the secret of being content in every situation, our hearts will not become bitter toward others who have more than we do or apathetic toward those who have less.

In one of their wittiest songs, Barenaked Ladies lists everything they'd buy if they had a million dollars. They'd buy cars (Reliant K cars, no less), monkeys, emus, and the remains of famous people. But they'd also eat Kraft dinners because, hey, they like them no matter what their bank statement says. When the song's big ending comes, they sum it all up with the profound point, "If I had a million dollars, I'd be rich."

We tend to think having a ton of money would change us dramatically—that our lives would be different if only we had more bucks! The Ladies are right: Yes, if we had a ton of money we'd be rich, but essentially we'd be the same people—or at least we should be.

Psalm 49:16-20 says,

Do not be overawed when a man grows rich,
    when the splendor of his house increases;
for he will take nothing with him when he dies,
    his splendor will not descend with him.
Though while he lived he counted himself blessed—
    and men praise you when you prosper—
he will join the generation of his fathers,
    who will never see the light of life.
A man who has riches without understanding
    is like the beasts that perish.

Isn't it amazing how others praise us when we prosper? Our world encourages us to evaluate God's blessing in our lives from the perspective of Wall Street. Yet God calls us to evaluate our lives by a different standard: to view success as living by faith and not the other way around.

The Nitty-Gritty

So we've looked at the overarching problem and our struggle to be content in the midst of our culture's attitude and pressure. Now let's look at what to do about our dilemma—practically.

Spending and Satisfaction

The best advice is simple: Spend within your means. We have become such a consumer- and debt-oriented society that we think it's natural to overspend. How many credit-card applications do you receive every month? Solicitations pour into our mailboxes, offering only 9 percent interest (to be upped to 17 percent after only a few months). When we buy into that system, we move into a downward spiral that can eat our lunch financially and keep us from having the time and money to do the things we most like and need to do.

Both of us often meet people in their late twenties who are still paying for decisions they made right after college. At the time they graduated, everything in them was screaming to buy a leather couch, an entertainment system, a fondue set, and embroidered flannel sheets (and this was *before* they'd received their first paycheck). So they went and plunked down five thousand dollars on a credit card, and it has taken them almost ten years to pay the debt off. A friend of mine (Doug's) went on a European bike-riding trip ten years ago that he completely bankrolled on his credit card. He and his wife are still paying interest on that venture.

The moral of these stories is simple: Don't, don't, don't spend more than you make. Pay off your credit card every month. Budget to buy things. Don't give your money away to credit-card companies and banks. Be careful with it so you can use it for the good of yourself and others. This one step will make a huge difference in your financial life.

If this advice comes too late, begin working now to eliminate the debt you've already accumulated. Consider consolidating your debt into one payment; you can usually find a company that will do this for you at a much lower interest rate than your credit card will give you. Cut back on some of your activities and expenses to devote that money to paying off your debts. This will be difficult, and you'll be tempted to blow it and give up, but realize that this will help set you free from the bondage of living on the credit side of life.[12]

The other piece of advice that goes along with all this can be even more difficult to follow: Resist the idea that you don't have enough and that more stuff or nicer stuff will make you happy. We're not saying that you should feel guilty for having nice things. We're saying (again) that you should avoid falling into a trap of making those nice things idols in your life.

After moving into our first house, Megan and I (Craig) had a gut check in this area when we went to buy a set of "real furniture."[13] The cushions of our hand-me-down gray sofa and love seat were splitting apart. Since we'd been having overnight guests sleep on an inflatable air mattress that kept losing air, we thought it would be a good time to invest in a sleeper sofa set.

We enjoyed our first trip to the furniture store. There were all kinds of new models and colors from which to choose for our living room. Finally, Megan found the "perfect" sleeper sofa, but the salesman told us that when special-ordered, safeguard sprayed, taxed, and delivered with just one other chair and no ottoman, this perfect sofa was going to cost us around eighteen hundred dollars. This was approximately a thousand dollars more than we had budgeted. We decided to keep looking.

We kept checking for sales and price drops for two months. Once we went back to the furniture store, prayed in the car for wisdom as to what to do about the sofa we wanted, and walked in only to see it "on sale" for five dollars less than the original price.

---

12. Otherwise known as "the Dark Side."
13. *Real furniture,* as it is defined here, consists of at least three separate pieces that match, does not include milk crates in any way, costs more than twenty-five dollars, is not inflatable, and is purchased in an actual store and not at a garage or yard sale.

Megan was in tears; I was frustrated. We weren't as disappointed about the price not dropping as we were by how much we had allowed ourselves to covet that one "perfect" sofa. We both knew we shouldn't get it, and yet we also knew we needed *something*. I went upstairs in the store because I remembered seeing one that I thought might work. As I rounded the corner, I saw it again, liked it still, and noticed that it was *really* on sale, unlike the other one. I *really* liked it then. I went back downstairs, got Megan, who liked it too, found a salesman, and began asking questions.

The answers were encouraging. Yes, the sofa came as a sleeper. Yes, all of the pieces for the entire set were in stock. Yes, they could deliver it that week. "Yes," I said. "We'll take it."

While Megan and I didn't get the perfect sofa we initially wanted, we got a far more kid-friendly sofa (as we've since found out in spades) for a thousand dollars less than we would have paid for a set with two fewer pieces. And we didn't go into debt. At first it was hard to say no to our champagne tastes, but ultimately it was good to say yes to the God-given discretion for which we had prayed earlier in the day. We were not just settling for something less-than; we were truly satisfied with what we got.

Saving and Investment

Getting our spending under control is one thing—and that's no easy task! But *saving* is another key factor in managing our money and our attitudes about finances. Reading *Kiplinger's* or *The Motley Fool* can dizzy you. In reality, saving can be much simpler than it sounds. The most important thing to know is that in our twenties we have time on our side—even our meager investments will add up. The little bit you do now will make a big difference later.

When I (Doug) was twenty-four and newly married, I had just started learning about money. I had been fairly careful with my spending, and I had a few hundred bucks sitting in a savings account. Then, during a ministry-training program, I met with my summer mentor, Jim, for the first time. "So, what mutual funds do you have?" was his first question. I'd been expecting something "spiritual," so I was caught off-guard. My answer: "What's a mutual fund?"

Jim then showed me a few things about investments, which is the next level of saving after you've saved up for emergencies. So I put some money into the mutual funds Jim suggested and started reading *Money* magazine so I could at least pick up the lingo and give my wife reason to have a little more financial confidence in me.

I learned that you can make mistakes in the market early on with fairly meager investments, but you'll already be ahead because you're making those mistakes in your twenties and learning from them early.

But how much is too much to save? Great question. We suppose it's different for everyone, but one principle that a friend shared with Craig is that we should always save toward something rather than just for the sake of seeing how much we can save. Identify the accounts, then you can figure up the amounts accordingly.

You do need some money stashed away so you aren't stuck when your car needs a new clutch, your washer blows up, or your friend needs you to drive to California tomorrow. A general fund of savings for such unplanned needs will help keep debt off your credit cards.

After that, you should establish a few reasonable medium-term goals and perhaps a few long-terms goals as well. Cars, vacations, houses, more education—these all hit our accounts with less disruption when there's already money there for them. It takes discipline and foresight to begin saving one hundred dollars a month for a future car, but after five years, that six thousand dollars feels pretty nice. Whether you put these savings in the bank or invest them in a less predictable but potentially more beneficial mutual fund is up to you. You should consider talking to a knowledgeable person in your church who can advise you on the different strategies.

We also know people who view their savings account or investments like the Harvard Endowment Fund. There's never enough in there. At that point, savings has become a security and identity issue. Remember, if you can't be content with what you have, no nest egg will ever satisfy you.

Giving and Fulfillment

K. P. Yohannan, director of the Gospel for Asia mission organization and author of the book *The Road to Reality*, writes about how many Americans spend more on their dogs or on keeping their lawns fertilized and watered than they do on foreign missions. We could cite statistics that show how lousy we are as a nation and a church at giving, but the issue is not one of finances so much as the heart.

One of the marks of discipleship is caring for the poor and needy (see James 1:27). In our twenties we need to cultivate the heart of a joyful giver, regardless of what we have or don't have. Most of us have more than we need, and all of us have more than most people in the world have. But the real reason to give can be found in 2 Corinthians 8:9: "For you know the grace of our Lord Jesus Christ, that though he was rich, yet for your sakes he became poor, so that you through his poverty might become rich."

When I (Craig) went to Africa, I sat in a Bible study with Ugandan students, each of whom lamented because he or she had not been taking initiative in sharing their meager resources of Bibles, books, and tapes with others. "I get a book, and I read the book," said Olga. "But when I'm done, I should give it to someone else who could then read it and pass it on as well. God is teaching me to be more generous."

Glancing at the floor, I thought about the hundreds of books Megan and I own, read, and keep on our shelves—not to mention the dozens of books we have on preorder with half.com, or the access we have to new and used bookstores in the United States. We are so Americanized in our understanding of sacrifice and giving that it's almost ridiculous when compared to how 80 percent of the world lives. I wondered what it would mean to live out Olga's generosity in my Colorado Springs culture.

John Wesley said, "Gain as much as you can; save as much as you can; give as much as you can." We can't really put it any better. Giving is the most important aspect of our money management—it will help every other thing we've talked about fall into place.

The idea of giving our money away can make us a bit queasy. Giving usually doesn't come as naturally as hoarding and spending. We think about how much we need and how much we want to have certain things. Then we rationalize that if we had a little more, we'd give a little more. We hear around Christmas that it is better to give than to receive, but it can be hard to live out that nicety—especially during the other eleven months of the year. How can our hearts change? How do we find joy in giving?

Our hearts will change when we acknowledge that God has given us everything and we are merely his stewards. We hold the trust of the things he owns. Realizing this makes it easier to give back to him the things that are his in the first place. C. S. Lewis tells the story of a man who wanted to buy his father a gift, so he went and asked his dad for the money to do so. When the father received the present from his son, he loved it, even though it hadn't brought any monetary value to his estate—if anything, it had taken some away. While the transaction hadn't benefited him in terms of commerce, the initiative of his loving son brought him delight.[14]

So it is with us. God has given us everything we have—not only our bank accounts, our sweaters, and our CDs but also our talents, our families, and our very lives. Anything we offer him is something he gave us. We see this concept played out over and over again in the book of Isaiah as the Israelites struggled with God's sovereign control of their nation. God continually assured Israel that he had a plan to restore the nation and that the real question wasn't What is going to happen? but Who is the One in charge? God is and was and will be the God of history and the Creator and Giver of all.

We should desire to incorporate giving into our everyday lives so that it simply *happens*. This is what the apostle Paul meant when he wrote, "Whoever sows sparingly will also reap sparingly, and whoever sows generously will also reap generously. Each man should give what he has decided in his heart to give, not reluctantly or under compulsion, for God loves a cheerful giver" (2 Corinthians 9:6-7). We are to give instinctively because we are so thankful for what we've been given.

But it isn't always so easy, is it? Our hearts must be right, for God loves a cheerful giver; but God also loves a *giver,* not one who constantly evaluates his or her heart and never gives at all. The fact is that sometimes obedience

---

14. C. S. Lewis, *Mere Christianity* (New York: HarperCollins, 2001).

begins the process of faith working in our hearts; other times it completes the process.

Regardless, it doesn't hurt to err on the side of being overly generous every now and then. So many times I (Doug) have passed by people begging in our big cities. For instance, every time I walked back to my car after a game at Busch Stadium (where the St. Louis Cardinals play baseball), I would see the same man. He sat in a wheelchair because he has no legs, and he has to use oxygen to aid his breathing. I had passed him dozens of times without stopping for even a second, but recently I started to pull out a buck or two when I went by. If one time—just one time—every person in the stadium gave him a dollar, he'd have $40,000 and maybe could start doing something better with his time and talents.

Now I can hear the objections already. He might spend it on alcohol or drugs or gamble it away on the lotto. You're right, we don't know what he would do with that money, but God cares about *my* response to him and not just *his* response to the money. Sure, he should be responsible with the dollar I give him, but it's not my job to run a credit check every time I give a buck away. I need to err more often than I do on the side of generosity instead of fiscal responsibility. Simply put: I need to give.

Our view of money shouldn't necessarily change if we have more or less of it. For example, if we are givers in our twenties when we have relatively little, we will be givers in our fifties when we're possibly farther up the ladder and earning bigger dollars. If we always long for more when we have an annual income of twenty thousand dollars, we will do the same when we earn two hundred thousand dollars. Dealing now with what we have or don't have is a great way to strengthen the financial foundation of our lives for later years.

Living Simply

Our world needs to be redeemed, not rejected. We don't redeem it when we place our trust and affections in the things of our world or reject the things of the world as being wrong. Instead, we redeem the world as we go out as

Christians and use things as they were intended to be used—for God's glory.[15]

Musician David Wilcox succinctly assesses our search for contentment in worldly things: "I mean when I've got everything I need…there's never enough."[16]

Money is "never enough" because it was never meant to be. God is the only One who can satisfy, the only One who can meet our longings for fulfillment. Realizing this brings tremendous freedom and peace and enables us to give and enjoy what God has so generously given to us. This is the Biblical Dream, and now is the time—in our twenties—to start dreaming it.

Ideas of Things to Do

- Read books about financial issues.
- Save up your money and wait to buy things later.
- Make a budget and stick to it.
- Don't accumulate credit cards. (You only need one.)
- Pay off your credit card every month. (So don't charge too much!)
- If you have debt already, think of creative ways to make and save more money. Set goals for how much you will be able to pay off each month.
- Resist the urge to think you always need something new.
- Buy clothes on sale or during their off-peak times.
- Take out loans only for big things—school, houses, and cars. Try not to take out a loan for the whole amount and attempt to make double payments if possible.
- Buy a home that fits your needs, not as a status symbol.

---

15. To see this contrast and how the things of our world can picture grace to others, watch the Danish film *Babette's Feast,* directed by Gabriel Axel (Denmark: 1987).
16. David Wilcox, "Never Enough," 1999. *Underneath,* Vanguard.

- Work fewer hours and make less money so you can have more time to volunteer for things you care about.
- Agree with your friends to live by biblical principles and use positive peer pressure to encourage one another to resist the world's temptations.
- Don't eat out as much.
- If you're married, decide to live off only one income and save the money from the second job. That way your standard of living won't climb higher and higher, and you'll have some money socked away when the time comes to buy the things you need.
- Ask for financial guidance from someone in your church who is older and has experience in that field.
- Read magazines to boost your knowledge base.
- Make car payments to yourself so you can build up a big down payment.
- Have banks automatically take money out of your account and put it into savings.
- Come up with a percentage for giving and take it off the top each week or month.
- Be a giver with your stuff too. Be generous with your house, your food, your possessions. Cultivate a generous heart.
- Tithe to your church and be involved with its mission.
- Pick one or two other ministries or missionaries you feel passionate about or know personally and give to them.
- Give your time. Be with people in need.
- Realize you are rich, abundantly blessed, and able to give to those who have less than you.
- Move in with others. You will save money (and experience community).
- Drive your car until it drops. Resist the idea that your car is a status symbol and something that gives you an identity. Use it for what it is: transportation.

- Go through your clothes and give away what you haven't worn in the past year.
- Check out movies at the library. (They're free, and you can keep them for a full week).

CHAPTER EIGHT

Time

USING (NOT JUST HAVING) THE TIME
OF OUR LIVES

*Once you become aware that the main business that you are here for is to
know God, most of life's problems fall into place of their own accord.*
—J. I. PACKER, *Knowing God*

Ruthlessly eliminate hurry.
—DALLAS WILLARD, in John Ortberg's *The Life You've Always Wanted*

Time or money. Which is more valuable to you?

Until a few years ago, if someone asked me (Doug) whether I wanted
to do a task myself or pay someone else to do it, I would say, "I have more time
than money" every time. I could afford twenty hours to paint a room, but not
to pay someone to do it. Slowly, though, that's changed. With four kids, I'd
rather pay someone to do some things than do them myself. Though I'm not
rich by any means, in many ways I have more money than time.

Time, not money, is the newest commodity of comparison among those
in their twenties. Both of us began to notice this in college when we asked how
others were doing, and they quickly gave us their latest schedule updates.
People weren't answering our questions about their well-being; they were
answering the question they thought would be more impressive: "So how busy
(and therefore important) are you?"

As you've no doubt experienced, one of the biggest struggles in our twenties is how we use our time, often because we fail to understand that time is a

gift. We need to learn to handle our time with stewardship, viewing it as no less valuable or fleeting than our money. Just as with money, we can idolize our schedules and our busyness or we can use our time for God and his glory.

We can easily be tempted to do the former. Recently someone asked me how my last few weeks had been. I answered just like I should try not to: summer conference in Florida, editing a book, wedding rehearsal then ceremony, preaching twice on Sunday, premarital counseling for another couple...whew. Even though that answer communicated something—Doug is tired and worn out and maybe cannot say no to people—it didn't answer the question my friend was asking.

The Puritans had a concept of *redeeming* time rather than *spending* time. This idea helps us think about how we use our time in our twenties. We need to learn now to redeem the time we've been given instead of just spending it. Spending time is particularly tragic because, unlike money, we can't reclaim it. In fact, wasting time quite literally means we are wasting our lives, and that's a scary proposition no matter how you think about it!

Some Mind-Blowing Considerations About Time

As we watch time pass, we try to develop new ways to make better use of it. But time itself can only be marked and measured, never prolonged or delayed. And although constant, time is also relative. Physicist Albert Einstein said, "When you are courting a nice girl an hour seems like a second. When you sit on a red-hot cinder a second seems like an hour."[1] The apostle Peter wrote, "With the Lord a day is like a thousand years, and a thousand years are like a day" (2 Peter 3:8). Because of its amazing properties—seemingly ever dynamic and yet static as the day is long—time is truly one of God's most mind-blowing concepts.

Another incredible reality check is that by the time we turn thirty we will have already lived a third of our lives, some of us perhaps even half. Living to the age of ninety (or even sixty) may seem unbelievable to us, but the idea of *not* living that long can be even more frightening. How can what once seemed

---

1. Albert Einstein, quoted in *News Chronicle*, 14 March 1949.

an *entire* lifetime when we were kids be *just* a lifetime only ten or fifteen years later? We become afraid not so much of dying but of dying without having accomplished anything important. We've yet to write that book we wanted to write or to travel around the world. We haven't had our first child, saved someone's life from tragedy, or been married. Sometimes we even wish our time here would end now rather than later, because we're so scared of merely existing with nothing to show for it.

In his book *Technics and Civilization,* Lewis Mumford writes of how the invention of the clock in the fourteenth century made us into timekeepers and then timesavers and now timeservers. He points out that once the clock came along, eternity ceased to serve as the measure and focus of human events; instead, the timepiece did. Neil Postman goes on to finish Mumford's observation:

> We have learned irreverence toward the sun and the seasons, for in a world made up of seconds and minutes, the authority of nature is superseded. The clock introduced a new form of conversation between man and God, in which God appears to have been the loser. Perhaps Moses should have included another commandment: Thou shalt not make mechanical representations of time.[2]

About five years ago I (Craig) stopped wearing a watch. Though I still needed to know on a daily basis what time it was, I gave up my timepiece for the simple reason that my preoccupation with it was turning me into a time legalist. Everything I did—brushing my teeth in the morning, meeting with someone for lunch, spending time with Megan—took on significance based on how much time I spent doing it. This silly little habit got to the point where I began breaking up the day not in terms of morning, afternoon, and evening or even by blocks of hours or individual hours themselves, but by minutes and sometimes even seconds. (I could brush my teeth in twenty-two seconds—not good for my teeth, nor for me to know that.)

---

2. Neil Postman, *Amusing Ourselves to Death* (New York: Viking, 1985), 11-2.

Time—not God—was the fixation of my life. And it showed. Sure, I was never late for appointments, but I wasn't much fun attending them either as they all seemed like unforgiving deadlines to me. Megan was glad when we got time together, but I was always thinking about the rest of my schedule and sometimes had trouble really enjoying those moments. None of this was healthy, and I finally recognized that I needed to take some steps to stop the cycle.

Today I still don't wear a watch, but I do check the time periodically on the handheld iPAQ I carry around. What's the difference? First, I have to work a little harder to pull the iPAQ out of my pocket to check the time; and second, since I took a break from always and easily glancing at my watch to see how late, early, or right on time I was, my perspective has changed. Now I try to consciously decide to use time as the gift it is rather than the curse I had made it to be.

Interruptions to Our Scheme of Things

When we view time as a punishment or prison or curse, we will probably view interruptions to our already-full schedules as negative surprises. Interruptions aren't always bad, though. God often takes pleasure in interrupting our plans to remind us that the details and schedules of our lives are not to distract us from him, the Giver of time. Interruptions often get us out of our harried routine just enough so we can hear the still, small voice of God.

My (Craig's) good friend Ken Bradbury once got pneumonia from staying up too late, getting up too early, teaching all day, writing and directing a musical all evening, and generally forgetting that he was human. Ken told me later that his sickness was the best thing that could have happened to him because he needed and wanted a break but didn't know how to schedule one for himself. God did it for him, though it entailed a week-long stay in the hospital, complete with hospital food. Now he's better at slowing down every now and then, but he still has a way to go. So do the rest of us.

Because so many things seem more urgent than they really are, it can be difficult to make the choice to read, write, and reflect—three keys to slowing down the pace of our lives. Our culture promotes the idea of working like crazy and then taking a short but intense vacation, which usually requires another vacation from that vacation (although we never seem to make the time to take that one). As we struggle in our twenties to get ahead in the workplace, the pressures of these expectations can be even more difficult to manage. If we slow down, work hard but less, pace ourselves and make time for other things, we may not be received too well by those above us who "paid their dues" to the same exhausting system. We may feel lazy or old-fashioned or wonder if we'll ever fit into a mentality that says "Go! Go! Go!"

Martin Luther once said, "I must make the personal confession that my own coming and going affects me and concerns me much more than the grace of our Lord Jesus Christ, as proclaimed in the gospel, comforts me."[3] How far we've come from the times of Luther, who ached at his preoccupation with his bustling sixteenth-century activities! What would he do if he had the Internet, ESPN, kids, workouts, telemarketers, and ten magazines a week delivered to his door begging for his attention? Like Luther, we may long for things spiritual, but the haze of our busy existence blinds us to the action such spirituality requires. Going to church, reading the Bible, praying, having others over for dinner to get to know them better—these all take time. Harder still, the payoff can seem too distant. Instead, deadlines and programs and activities have a much harder edge, as "I'm late for a meeting" can sound more legitimate to our crazed culture than "I'm late for my time with the Lord."

Spending intentional time with God in obedience to him costs us other opportunities—we could always be doing something else. But as J. Oswald Sanders said, "We are at this moment as close to God as we really choose to be."[4] In other words, not only do we have to have good intentions about getting close to God, we have to follow through. As John Townsend and Henry Cloud write in their book *Boundaries,* "In life, we always end up experiencing

---

3. Martin Luther, *Sermons of Martin Luther, The House Postils,* vol. 1 (Grand Rapids: Baker, 1996), 66.
4. J. Oswald Sanders, *Enjoying Intimacy with God* (Grand Rapids: Discovery House, 2000), 12.

what we tolerate."[5] Our intentions rarely become more than wishes unless we are disciplined. And turning our intentions into reality is the key to making good use of our time.

Discipline and the Disciplines

While *freedom* and *personal rights* are the buzzwords of our culture today, we don't hear much about words such as *accountability* and *discipline*. Sure, when someone breaks the law in a big and public way, there's a call for accountability, and when the Olympics come around every four years, we watch a series of vignettes about an athlete's discipline to get there. But that's about it. In fact, our society often promotes the idea that we shouldn't be held responsible for anything. We're victims of aggressive drivers, bad information, and fat grams. Nothing is said of our own choice to do or not do something.

At times we both have wanted to scrap the whole idea of a disciplined life in exchange for the free-and-easy one that our culture promotes. Who hasn't? But the Spirit of God reminds us that "no discipline seems pleasant at the time, but painful. Later on, however, it produces a harvest of righteousness and peace for those who have been trained by it" (Hebrews 12:11). Not only that, Proverbs 5:23 says, "He will die for lack of discipline, led astray by his own great folly."

Since we both have small children, we're familiar with the process of teaching kids to read. It's hard work to practice sounding out the letters and new word combinations every day. Most kids want to give up at some point (we won't even go into what the parents sometimes want!). It's too hard. It takes too much time. But "no discipline seems pleasant at the time." Learning to read becomes one of the greatest things a child can discover. Giving up on that process has incredible consequences. We (and our wives) persevere to help our kids see the "harvest"—being able to read whatever they want on their own—and do our best to model and provide enough discipline for them to get there.

---

5. Henry Cloud and John Townsend, *Boundaries,* rev. ed. (Grand Rapids: Zondervan, 1992).

Knowing God better doesn't have to be any more mysterious than succeeding in daily activities like reading, exercise, or dieting. But it does take a certain measure of discipline. Many specific disciplines have a place in the Christian life—fasting, celebration, meditation, and solitude, for example. We'd like to focus in this chapter on four of these disciplines: prayer, Bible reading, Scripture memorization, and community participation.

We encourage you to think about how these disciplines can become a bigger part of your use of time every day. First, though, a word of caution: I (Doug) used to approach these disciplines with my long and involved prayer card, my quiet times checked off every day for a year, a bulging verse pack of memorized Scriptures, and a front-row seat at church each and every Sunday. I taught them this way, hoping that people would feel guilty for not being spiritual (like me) or devoted (like me) or possibly even a Christian (of course, like me). Anything wrong with this picture? Motivation by guilt, while perhaps effective in the short term, isn't good enough for most of us in the long term. Why? Because, as author Jerry Bridges writes, "Discipline without desire is drudgery."[6]

We develop in the disciplines *because* God approves of us, not to *gain* his approval. Our pride should be in Christ and his pursuit of us, not in ourselves and our pursuit of him. We have to remember that our first-level identity is not in question here: God loves us as his children. We're just trying to answer the question, How can we know him better? Let's consider these disciplines in more detail.

Prayer: Talking All the Time

Back in about A.D. 397, Augustine of Hippo penned these words,

> You, my God, are supreme, utmost in goodness, mightiest and all-powerful, most merciful and most just. You are the most hidden from us and yet the most present among us, the most beautiful and yet the most strong, ever enduring and yet we cannot comprehend you. You

---

6. Jerry Bridges, *The Discipline of Grace* (Colorado Springs: NavPress, 1994), 24.

are unchangeable and yet you change all things. You are never new, never old, and yet all things have new life from you.... We give abundantly to you so that we may deserve a reward, yet which of us has anything that does not come from you? You repay us what we deserve, and yet you owe nothing to any. You release us from our debts, but you lose nothing thereby. You are my God, my Life, my holy Delight, but is this enough to say of you? Can any man say enough when he speaks of you? Yet woe betide those who are silent about you! For even those who are most gifted with speech cannot find words to describe you.[7]

Prayer is a privilege. It is an opportunity to converse with the "mightiest and all-powerful, most merciful and most just" Creator. Prayer is, in its simplest form, talking with God. We can come to God any time of the day, in any place, and in any situation to talk to him. Prayer can be formal or casual, quick or long, private or public. We know this. And yet we so often neglect to pray. We get too busy, too involved, too self-sufficient. We need to remember, however, that we *get* to pray more than we *have* to pray. God allows us to communicate with him.

Sometimes starting or renewing your prayer life means coming back to the meaning of the words we say and the fact that we can say them so freely. You'll remember that Jesus himself taught us to pray in what we call the Lord's Prayer (Matthew 6:9-13). This prayer briefly covers all the bases of our communication to God—recognizing that he is the Creator and Ruler of the world, being thankful that he provides for our needs, expressing our need for forgiveness, and petitioning him for protection from evil. This prayer is probably familiar to you, either from your childhood Sunday school classes or from your current church services. Be wary, though, of memorizing it and then forgetting what you're saying. Every now and then when we pray the Lord's Prayer at night, I (Doug) ask my kids, "Now what are 'debts'? What is 'our daily bread'? What does, 'Your kingdom come' mean?" This helps us remember what it is we're saying rather than merely chanting the words.

---

7. Augustine of Hippo, *Confessions* (bk. 1, sec. 4).

Another place to go to learn about prayer is John 17, where Jesus prayed before his death. Before he went to the cross to pay for our sins, Jesus prayed for himself, for his disciples, and for all his people everywhere. What a time of devotion to his Father and a chance for us to see his heart right before he died.

One thing I like to do is use Scripture—the very words of God—to pray. If I'm praying about resisting temptation in a certain area of my life, for example, I might pray,

> Lord, you know I'm having a lot of trouble lately in this area and I
> need your help. You say that you won't let me be tempted beyond what
> I can bear. That's hard for me to believe right now since I'm right in
> the middle of it, but I believe what you say is true, and I know you can
> give me the strength to persevere and get out of this. I know that Jesus
> fought and beat this type of temptation, and that gives me hope since
> he lives for me. Help me seize the moment when I see that you've pro-
> vided a way out so that I can stand up under it. I know you care about
> me so much and don't want me to fail. Forgive me for my weakness
> and help me to be strong that I might give you glory.

If you look up 1 Corinthians 10:13, you can see that this verse is woven into my prayer, helping me to know I'm on the right track since I'm using Scripture itself to guide my word choice. The thing is, God hears all of our prayers and knows their true meaning, and he answers our prayers out of an awareness of our hearts, so we don't have to worry about praying just "right." He loves to talk with his children.

As you pray, listen for God. Be quiet and try to discern how he might be directing your heart. This takes time. You may not hear an audible voice, but after a while you may feel a calming of your soul as God floods you with his perfect peace. Or you may feel a disturbance in your soul and a breaking of your spirit as you realize you have been in sin and not realized it. That is the work of the Holy Spirit in you.

One of my seminary professors said to me, "Blessed is the man who never stops starting family devotions." That stuck with me. Our family has seasons when we pray well and often, read the Bible together with passion, and memorize catechism answers together. But then we go through seasons when none of those things happen. We travel on Sunday nights and miss a few times. We lose our hymnal. We're tired and don't pay attention. We need to begin again and seek God's face together.

Just as we should never stop starting family devotions, we shouldn't stop starting with our prayer life. If you're drifting away from a growing prayer life, snap back. Begin anew to seek your Savior's face through prayer. It's a privilege.

Bible Reading: More than a Bestseller

Bible reading is another privilege God provides for us that we often take for granted. But we often have to begin it again and again.

If you're trying to make time to get into the Scriptures on your own, you can find all sorts of plans out there for reading the Bible: the *One Year Bible*, the *One Minute Bible*, the *Radioactive Genius Alien Plumber's Bible*, and who knows what else. Whichever you choose, you need to find the plan that works best for you and stick with it, starting up again when you've stopped.

Reading the Bible can be a daunting task as you start flipping through the pages and read names of people like Nebuchadnezzar and Maher-Shalal-Hash-Baz.[8] You're buzzing along and then start to read about how many bowls the Israelites bought and how many shields and how many donkeys, and that goes on for thirty pages! You keep going and start to find out that if you have mold in your clothes, there's an elaborate process for discerning if it's legitimate or not. Then there's the history of a people and their friends and enemies and territories that all have faded into history and are a bit tough to keep straight. Almost every reader is baffled at some point by this completely different vocabulary, history, and story structure.

Whew. What are we to do? "Never, never, never give up," as Winston Churchill would say (albeit in a different context). Keep going, keep plugging away. This book is not just any book, but the actual Word of God, the inspired Scripture of what he wants us to know about him, about his people, and about

---

8. Isaiah's son (see Isaiah 8:1,3).

the way he works in the world. It's worth our time and energy. In our twenties we can set a pattern for study and devotion to the Bible that will carry us the rest of our lives.

I (Craig) have approached the Bible in several different ways throughout my life so far. In high school I said I believed it, though I had little idea what it really said. In college I got really excited about studying and memorizing it but kind of used what I was learning to club myself and others. After graduation I was involved in a variety of different studies on numerous topics, which was great, but I tended to make the prep work purely academic, thereby missing the voice of the One who wrote it.

Now that I'm married and have kids, it takes real intention to find time to read the Scriptures, let alone to study or memorize them. In fact, there have been periods of time—more than I care to admit—during which I couldn't have told you where my Bible was because I hadn't seen it in weeks. That's sometimes how reading the Bible goes. We stop doing it, we realize we miss it, we find our Bibles, and then we start reading them again, listening more closely for that still, small Voice we've not heard recently and asking God for a new desire to desire his Word. It's hard. It's glorious. It's a pain. But it's what we need.

Perhaps you've misplaced your trusty *Precious Moments Bible* in your latest move and need a new one. We'd suggest you buy a translation of the Bible that is faithful to the original language and fairly easy to understand. The *New International Version* (NIV), the *English Standard Version* (ESV), and the *New American Standard Bible* (NASB) are high on our lists. Whether you're starting or starting again to read Scripture, you might consider reading first the letters of Paul (Romans, 1 and 2 Corinthians, Galatians, Ephesians, Philippians, Colossians, 1 and 2 Timothy, Titus, and Philemon) since they're fairly straightforward. The Gospels (Matthew, Mark, Luke, and John) and Acts are good too, as they give firsthand accounts of the life of Christ.

Wherever you dig in, try to read at two levels: for breadth and for depth. Reading for breadth means reading just to get the story, to see what happens, to follow the flow of the book and to make those top-level observations. You can get a lot out of this type of reading. Reading for depth means taking a step below the surface and getting out a Bible dictionary or concordance or even a commentary to figure out what some of the less obvious things mean. What are the various words for "love" in New Testament times, and how can we know which one is meant here? What is a "talent"? Why would Jesus' turning water into wine be something to include in his story? What is a legion of soldiers? What does it mean in John 1:14 that Jesus "made his dwelling among us"? Ask questions of the text and then take those questions to the books you've checked out or bought. Ask your Christian friends and your pastor what they think too.

As you grow in confidence and consistency, move on to some of the tougher books in the Old Testament and experience the richness of God's grace there as well. You may have read them long ago but haven't visited them in a while. Both of us are continually amazed at how much we learn each time we read these books again. You will be too.

Don't fall into the temptation of thinking that the New Testament is cool while the Old Testament is boring, or that the New Testament shows the God of grace while the Old Testament reveals the God of the Law. Those are false dichotomies. Search for grace in the Old Testament and law in the New Testament. Trace a theme through the Bible. Read one book at a time all the way through so you can see the themes in it. Don't open your Bible randomly, but have a small plan in place when you read (for example: Genesis then Matthew then Exodus then Mark, etc.). Make notes in your Bible in the margins, underline verses that stand out to you that you want to share with someone later. Journal your thoughts when you're confused or challenged or excited. Get in a Bible study with others who want to learn so that you can learn together.

This is exciting stuff. Consistent Bible reading helps us know our God better, the One who created us and redeemed us. Knowing what he's about is a good idea—do whatever you can to get into his Book!

Scripture Memorization: Filling Our Heads with More than Filler
One of the most beneficial disciplines we both started in our early twenties was memorizing Bible verses. I (Doug) didn't have a grand plan at first, though I did have visions of quoting entire books and blocks of books on demand. I

didn't quite get there, but I did find out that every verse I memorized got into my head so much that it seemed to become a part of me. When we steel our minds and capture the very words of Scripture in our hearts, we are better prepared for the trials ahead, and we can meditate on the Bible all day long without even having to have the book in our hands.

Jesus knew the Bible. He quoted Scripture when he was being tempted by Satan in the wilderness (Matthew 4:1-11). David said that he had hidden God's Word in his heart that he might not sin (Psalm 119:11). Solomon wrote that those learning the faith should guard the teaching as the apple of their eye, writing it on the tablets of their hearts (Proverbs 7:2-3). Memorizing Scripture gives us greater confidence in times of suffering or when we are wondering what the Lord would have us do. If you commit Scripture to mind, you'll find that a verse will often come to mind just when you need it, and you'll have comfort or courage or an answer or a heart for someone in need.

Memorizing Scripture also allows us to meditate on the Word of God. As the Israelites were about to enter the Promised Land, Joshua told them, "Do not let this Book of the Law depart from your mouth; meditate on it day and night, so that you may be careful to do everything written in it" (Joshua 1:8). The Israelites were to be centered on God's instructions so they would know where they needed to go and how they should think about God.

The word *meditate* means "to chew, to mull, to figure out, to consider what something means, to turn it over in your mind." When you meditate, noises might come out of your mouth like "hmmmm" or "ohh?!" and people will probably look at you strangely. Emphasizing different words can facilitate this meditation. For example, if we were meditating on Joshua 1:8, we might say to ourselves, "Do NOT let this Book of the LAW depart from your mouth; MEDITATE on it day AND night, so that you MAY be careful to DO everything written in it." This might get us thinking (hmmmm....): What does it mean to meditate day AND night? How MAY I then be careful to do everything written in it? As you meditate and mull that over in your mind, you may begin to see parts of the verse you hadn't considered before.

As you continue to memorize and meditate on the Scriptures, put yourself in the shoes of the writer or the original listener. What would you see or feel or think about these things? What picture do you think of when you see Joshua stepping into the Jordan River with the ark and a nation behind him and big scary people in the land before him? Where does your mind go when you think of the lepers Jesus healed who didn't come back to thank him? What was the Garden of Eden like? What will the new garden described in Revelation be like?

These are things you can think about in the bathtub or playing racquetball or waiting at a kids' swim meet because you have the Scripture memorized and right there in your head. How do you do it? It's not hard, but it takes some practice, some stick-to-it-iveness, and some accountability.

We suggest that you buy The Navigators' *Topical Memory System* (TMS). It's a great way to get started on memorizing verses in a systematic way. But if you don't want to get it, here's all it is: sixty important verses printed on little cards. Big deal, but it takes a bit of work to put your own version all together by writing out the cards (you can do it on three-by-five index cards or print them on your computer) and figuring out what verses to put on them. The TMS at least helps by giving you a little kit that does it all for you. You can easily keep going from there with your own topics and verses.

However you get verses on cards, once you have them down, carry them around with you (to work, in the car, to the store, but *not* to the shower) and pull them out whenever you have a free second. Go over the verse, assigning it a topic to help you recall it (for example: Love, God's Faithfulness, My Sinfulness, The Covenant, Lust) and the reference (Revelation 7:9). Then begin getting the verse in your mind part by part. Repeat the part you know and then add a few more words until you have it. The reference can be easy to forget, so it's best to say it once at the beginning and once at the end.

The key to keeping your verses sharp in your mind isn't in memorizing them right away. It's in reviewing them fairly often so you won't forget the last one when you move on to the next one. To do this, before you start on your newest verse, pull out a few that you memorized before and review them. After you pile up a few, you'll have to come up with a system for review in order to get through them all in a week or a month so you won't forget.

Remember: It's not how many verses you have that are important; it's how many verses "have" you as you meditate on them and put them into practice. Pray that God will use these to transform you as you begin to replace the pictures you have in your mind (think of an art gallery with a variety of paintings and photographs ranging from beauty to smut) with new images that comply with Philippians 4:8: "Whatever is true, whatever is noble, whatever is right, whatever is pure, whatever is lovely, whatever is admirable—if anything is excellent or praiseworthy—think about such things." It's also helpful to enlist others to join with you so you can review the verses together and ask each other what it is that you're learning from what you've memorized.

You and Me: Disciplined Together
Some people may not think of community as a discipline (that is, something we have to be self-controlled to do), but for others, the practice of community presence is a huge challenge.

We know people who think that if they just do the above disciplines—"just me and Jesus"—they'll be fine. But God tells us differently in the Bible. He says that we aren't so much individuals all out there seeking Christ as much as we are a body, a community seeking Christ *together*. We're bonded *together*. We're in relationship. We'll talk more about this in chapter 10, but it bears mentioning here and now.

Hebrews 10:24-25 says, "And let us consider how we may spur one another on toward love and good deeds. Let us not give up meeting together, as some are in the habit of doing, but let us encourage one another—and all the more as you see the Day approaching." God has put us in a body of believers and collectively called us his bride. You can't really be faithful to God and to the Bible until you are in relationship with others who are seeking to do the same.

Pray, read the Bible, and memorize Scripture with others, spur one another on. Discipline yourself to go to church on Sunday for worship. Get in a small group with other Christians. To do any and all of this takes time and energy and doesn't "just happen." But in our twenties we often become too self-focused and self-referential for our own good. We really do need others to speak into our lives and walk alongside us to keep us on track. Remembering that we are one part of a body and pursuing the other parts in that body is a discipline no less important than the others.

Well, It's About Time

You may not feel as if you have much time these days, but remember: Time is relative! Believe it or not, in our twenties we probably have more time to practice the disciplines than we will in the later decades of our lives.

Our struggle is not as much a matter of time management as it is of priority management. This sounds simple enough, but our culture does us a disservice by pluralizing the word *priority,* confusing us as to what our priorities are and should be. Think about it: When we talk about our priorities, we're talking about something that doesn't make sense—remember, the nature of priority is singular, not plural! We are only able to have *one priority.* The decision we have to make, then, is what that one priority is going to be.

Making the most of the minutes we've been given will not always come easily, but if we faithfully begin to incorporate prayer, Bible reading, Scripture memory, and community into our lives, we will be in a better position to understand and hear God's voice each day. This is not only essential for the good of our souls and our worldviews; it is the only way to discern what is truly worthy of our time.

Hundreds of books have been written on time management and time-saving techniques, but here is the bottom line for us: Time is a gift given to us by God. We should take care to use it wisely and intentionally, not fretting over every second we lose, but also not taking for granted how we will redeem each day we have been given. Take some time to think about that.

Ideas of Things to Do

- Take personal retreats. Go away by yourself and spend the day with God. Take your Bible and a journal and maybe a devotional book and simply sit and be still. Listen to God. Pray over the lists you have made. Talk out loud and have a real conversation with your Maker and Redeemer. Linger over the Scriptures.

- Take prayer walks. Involving your legs and your mind gives a slightly different dimension to your prayers. Get out and walk around your neighborhood or outside your office, praying for the people in the buildings as you pass by.
- Use your time in the car for Scripture memory or prayer or listening to teaching tapes. Car time can be so wasted on talk radio, top forty, and what the latest trade rumors are for the shortstop on your favorite baseball team. Some of that is fine, but be aware that your time could also be redeemed in ways that might be more helpful.
- Read good books. (We recommend some classics in the back of this book.)
- Get involved at your church. Be there. Get in a small group. Invite others to pray with you and read the Bible with you. Attend a conference now and then to expand your learning.
- Go a day (a week? a year?) without a watch, and learn to structure your days in other ways.
- Make a "stop-doing" list, and stop doing what you write down as your time wasters.
- Don't complain about how little time you have, and don't let others do it around you either. Instead, focus on talking about how you're investing your time and what you expect the fruits of that investment will one day be.
- Set parameters when you meet with people. If you really only have thirty minutes, tell them so and leave on time so they understand you're serious about redeeming your time.
- Don't waste others' time; instead respect it by not being late to appointments.
- Put together a time budget.
- Plan blocks of uninterrupted time so you can focus and get done what you need to get done.
- Stop believing the lie that you are important because of all you do.

CHAPTER NINE

Love: The Significance
of "Significant Other"

Love until it hurts. Real love is always painful and hurts.
Then it is real and pure.
—MOTHER TERESA

Some people call me the Space Cowboy
Some call me the Gangster of Love
—STEVE MILLER BAND, "The Joker"

I (Craig) will never forget my first date. It was summer; I'd had my license for roughly four months and was driving the ultimate love machine—a four-door, salmon-colored '84 Oldsmobile Delta 88 and former family car that my parents had passed on to me. I put in a cassette of U2's *The Joshua Tree*, pulled out of our gravel lane onto the Griggsville–New Salem blacktop, and began imagining how great this evening was going to be. The music was loud, the year was 1987, and I was a poster child for love.

Suddenly, and with no warning, a renegade fly that had stowed away aboard my stylish land yacht attacked me. In a compulsive panic I rolled down the window and began trying to swat the fly out. In doing so, I lost control of the car, veered off the right side of the road, and plunged the newly washed Olds into a fourteen-foot ditch, landing it hard on the passenger side and almost flipping it over on its top. As Bono started singing "Where the Streets Have No Name,"[1]

---

1. Consider the irony here. I'm not making this up.

I found myself hanging by my seat belt from what was now the top of the car, looking down and to my right at a smashed passenger-side window with grass shooting up through it. I remember hoping that the fly had died a terrible death in the whole ordeal. I also remember wondering how this could be love when I was just a mile and a half from home in a totaled car on its side in a ditch?

Believe it or not, I still went on the date. After catching a ride home from a neighbor and explaining to my parents what happened, I called Deb to tell her about my wreck and that I still wanted to get together. I then called my good friend, Peg Ratliff, and asked her to drive me the forty-five minutes to Jacksonville. It ended up being a good evening.

As I look back, I see two important life lessons as a result of my first-date experience: (1) a fly can't hurt you as much as a potentially fatal car wreck can, and (2) the pursuit of love often means leaving your wrecked car in the ditch, swallowing your pride, and going to the movies anyway.

First Kisses, First Struggles

Love is a many-splendored thing, or so the song goes. It can also be very exciting, frustrating, enamoring, repulsing, blind-siding, all-consuming, heart-melting, heartbreaking, and amazing. Love has been the topic of more books, songs, magazine articles, and made-for-TV movies than probably any other topic in the history of the world. No topic intrigues us as much as love.

Perhaps a first kiss started us on a journey through the craziness of romance—or perhaps it has come to epitomize the angst of it all. My (Doug's) first kissing *attempt* was in fifth grade, during which time I schemed to take Angie to the other side of the tracks where we'd have a little more privacy. After eighteen minutes of getting up the nerve and steeling my sense of purpose, I convinced her to set out—just as we ran into the teacher who said that recess was over. Denied.

My first *actual* kiss came a few years later in a Truth or Dare game I lost. I had to (got to) kiss Stacey for a full timed minute. Cool. Even cooler was the giddy exhilaration I felt when our lips met, time passed, and I realized that I had just kissed a girl on the mouth for the first time. I tell you all this not to extol the merits of Truth or Dare but to illustrate how moments like these stick out in our memories because they encompass so much of who we are physically, mentally, emotionally, and intellectually.

What do you remember? It's important to think about it a bit because how we deal with issues of relationships, romance, and sex hinges on our personal experiences. For instance, when I (Craig) was a kid, I attended a lot of weddings of family friends and neighbors. For whatever reason, I distinctly remember marveling at how two people could stand in front of a crowd of three hundred and kiss each other—and on the lips! Then when I found out what traditionally went on later that evening on the honeymoon, I was at a loss as to how two grown adults could shake hands with all those people at their reception when *they* knew that all the *people* knew just what it was they were going to be doing in a few hours. This thought was painfully embarrassing for me, and I wasn't even the one getting married!

This kind of embarrassment later developed into a hesitancy to show physical affection in public. Now, while it has nothing to do with her, Megan still has to remind me that it's okay for me to put my arm around her or to hold her hand in front of other people. Because of some of my experiences growing up, it's taken some time for me to really feel comfortable doing that. I don't know why I was that way, but once I got it in my head, it became part of my worldview. It's something I've had to outgrow.

One more example of our backgrounds affecting our futures: I (Doug) am not sure where I got it, but I developed a terrible attitude toward girls in high school. My mantra was: "Guys are jerks. Girls are stupid. Relationships stink." Although I longed for relationships with the opposite sex as a validation of my personhood, I tapped into all of the wrong ideas that the media feeds us about what makes a real man—macho, sarcastic, powerful, uncaring. My lanky body and huge Adam's apple didn't help me much, so I tried to overcome those undesirable features with a quick wit, a sharp tongue, and constant overachievement. This led me to feel superior, often demeaning the women around me.

I'm ashamed of all this, but that's where I was when I came to better understand the gospel in college. From that point I either was in absolute awe of women (I was meeting so many amazing ones!), or I ran from them to avoid thinking about the subject at all. Thus when I met Julie in the dorm cafeteria, I was pretty messed up, though you wouldn't know it from looking at me since I was a "well-adjusted" Midwestern boy. In reality, I didn't have a clue about relationships, and most of what I had learned didn't help me know how to treat and respect women. Thankfully, God really worked with Julie and me. Though we made a lot of dating mistakes, we ended up committed and faithful to each other, and the Lord saw us through to marriage.

We all pick up ideas about what a man or woman is or does. Some of those thoughts can be helpful for us, and others can give us misleading perceptions. Our twenties are a good time to pick through what we've learned and what God says about the differences between men and women and how we should come together to complement each other.

The Difference Between
Genesis 2 and Genesis 3

A funny thing happens as twentysomethings work out our relationships—an amazing number of us get married. However, an increasing number of people didn't have a good marriage modeled for them growing up, or they experienced abuse or divorce from the people who loved them the most. Throw in a fair share of rejection through junior high, high school, and college, and you've got a recipe for across-the-board relational dysfunction. Yet we still long for relationship. Whether or not we end up walking down the aisle, most of us are inexplicably drawn to the idea of long-term love.

So why is it so hard to line up relationships with our longings? For one thing, in our culture of nonabsolutes, terms that used to mean one thing can now mean a variety of things. For instance, *commitment* used to mean "until death us do part." Now *commitment* suggests "until something better comes along." The word *forever* used to mean "a time that never ends." Now *forever* refers to a period of time that fits in between two other ones (for example, "I love you forever now, but that may change if I feel differently later"). With this vernacular in place, is it any wonder that our culture's understanding of love is in the shambles that it is?

God did have a picture in mind when he designed relationships between men and women. The Bible offers us some encouraging pictures so we can focus on the good as a vision for the future. Let's start with Genesis and look at Adam and Eve.

Read Genesis 1 quickly. What strikes you? God created everything. We have a manifesto here, the introduction to a magnificent symphony of God's work in the world. "In the beginning, God created the heavens and the earth" (verse 1). As we read the descriptions of that creation, we read over and over again, "And God saw that it was good" (verses 10,12,18,21,25). Everything God created was good. At the end of the chapter, God created people and gave us the mandate to be creative as we cultivate and care for the earth. He looked at us and said, "And it was very good" (verse 31). Not just good but *very* good. Then he rested.

In Genesis 2 the spotlight turns back to Day Six, the People Day. Before we read about Adam's activities, we get the first indication that all is not well with the world. Something is "not good." In Genesis 2:18 we read, "The LORD God said, 'It is not good for the man to be alone. I will make a helper suitable for him.'" Both a man and a woman must be created to fully reflect God's image and his delight. Man must have someone like him so he can experience some of the same relational intimacy of the Trinity.

It's then that we read about Adam's tootling around naming everything ("octopus," "espresso," "jumping jacks," "baseball," "Coke Classic," etc.). We get the idea that he started to wonder about these pairs he kept seeing: *What's the deal with these slightly different animals, and why don't I have a slightly different person, someone who helps me do this naming stuff?* God loved Adam so much that he created the perfect match for him, a person who complemented him in every way. He created her from Adam's rib, a place so very close to Adam's heart, and Adam woke up saying, "Whoa! Man!" Or more specifically, he said, "This is now bone of my bones and flesh of my flesh; she shall be called 'woman,' for she was taken out of man" (Genesis 2:23). He recognized that, all of a sudden, he and Eve were in this together. The very next thing written is, "For this reason a man will leave his father and mother and be united to his wife, and they will become one flesh. The man and his wife were both naked, and they felt no shame" (verses 24-25).

These are amazing verses. They tell us about the first love story between a man and a woman who were thrilled with each other, who were pumped about their partnership and psyched about what was about to happen physically as well. Genesis 2 provides a beautiful vision of the way things are meant to be in marriage. So why isn't this our experience today? In Genesis 3 we read about why we struggle so much in this area, why we're so confused and angry, why we reject God's good gift and turn it into exploitation. Adam and Eve made a choice to sin, and we have been following in their footsteps ever since. Our sinful nature influences every relationship we have, especially our most important one.

After Genesis 3 we don't see too many pictures of healthy families or marriages in the Bible. In fact, most of the leaders of the Bible struggled in this area, which shows us just how powerful that fall into sin really was. The Song of Songs in the Old Testament, however, gives a positive picture of romantic, marital love. Though it sounds a bit foreign to our ears because it's written in Middle Eastern thought,[2] this is a book with some graphic sexual imagery. And the book of Ruth has a fantastic love story between Ruth and Boaz that depicts a fascinating, heart-stopping picture of risk taking and sacrifice.

With this reality check in mind, we might be tempted to wonder if love is worth it. After all, doesn't everyone get burned anyway at some point in time? But God promises to restore our relationship with him and with one another as a result of our salvation. That's part of the tough work of sanctification, but God can redeem our relationships even though we're still messed up people. He offers us grace so that we might again experience the true joys of love as sacrificial people. This is who we want to be and where we want to go, but how do we become that and get there?

---

2. We wouldn't try flocks of goats, fawns, goblets, pomegranates, or sheep as descriptions of our "valentine" today.

The Three Rights

As you seek to answer the question, Who am I? you may notice someone of the opposite sex beside you who is trying to do the same thing. Hmmmm. Could this be the person God has intended for you to marry? Perhaps? Please? Now is the time to consider the Three Rights: the Right Person in the Right Way at the Right Time.[3]

The Right Person

Begin with the Right Person (notice we didn't say the *Perfect* Person). Why is he so special to you? What qualities does she have that you most admire? What are the things about him or her that bring out the best in you? Thinking through these questions will help you sort out the qualities you're looking for and how they stack up with the person you desire.

When we were in college, we both made lists that described the kind of girl we thought we wanted to marry. While our lists were quite different from each other's in the little things (hair color, degree of athleticism, height, etc.), they lined up pretty closely on the big things (deep relationship with God, strong heart for people, love of children, etc.). We weren't trying to be mean or demeaning with our lists; we just needed to start somewhere in identifying who we thought the Right Person for each of us might be.[4]

As we met and befriended different women on campus, we wanted to enjoy their friendship. Along the way we sometimes wondered about the prospect of pursuing them romantically. As we evaluated them against our lists, many didn't stack up to what we thought we wanted because they weren't interested in a deep relationship with God, which was our number one priority. Others loved Jesus, but our personalities and visions for our lives didn't mesh. It was helpful to have some kind of criteria to evaluate our

---

3. We heard this thought originally from Larry Glabe, a Navigators campus minister at Mizzou at the time who now leads a community ministry there.
4. We weren't only *looking* for the Right Person, but we were also trying to *become* the Right Person for someone else. You shouldn't expect to find a woman of God unless you are serious about being a man of God—and vice versa.

compatibility and not just a warm, gushy feeling that ebbed and flowed in direct relation to our hormones.[5]

As we later met and got to know the two women who eventually became our wives, we realized that not only did they fit most of the initial descriptions of who and what we thought we were looking for, they actually began to *redefine* some of our peripheral definitions. Their qualities became *the* qualities that really attracted us. In other words, our *preferred* hair color (Craig: brown; Doug: red) simply defaulted to be *their* hair color (Megan: blonde; Julie: brown). Small (and silly) things didn't matter because we were enamored with who they were and who they were becoming. Megan and Julie were seeking to answer the same question we were (Who am I?), and we liked the answers we all seemed to be coming up with. We were each the Right Person for the other, and this fact gave us freedom to move forward with intention.

The Right Way

In Genesis 24 Abraham sent his servant to find a wife for his son Isaac. The servant, a bit daunted by his task, asked God for success and put together his own list (granted, a bit Old Testament-ish when compared to ours, but a list nonetheless)[6] of how he would determine the Right Person for Isaac. He set off with high hopes, traveled a bit, saw Rebekah at the well, and hurried to meet her. He first asked her for water. Now look at how he went about evaluating whether she was "the one": "*Without saying a word,* the man watched her closely to learn whether or not the Lord had made his journey successful" (Genesis 24:21, emphasis added).

He watched her—in her context and without making his objectives known at the time—to learn whether or not *the Lord* had made his journey successful. Had things gone south in terms of expectations (if she had drawn the water and poured it over his head), nothing would have been lost, because

---

5. It sure was a lot messier than it sounds in this paragraph. We don't want to give you the wrong impression that this was easy by any means.
6. "May it be that when I say to a girl, 'Please let down your jar that I may have a drink,' and she says, 'Drink, and I'll water your camels too'—let her be the one you have chosen for your servant Isaac" (Genesis 24:14).

he had not communicated his intentions to her. Nobody would get hurt (although he might have gotten a little wet), and the servant and Rebekah could go about their business without any real damage done.

This, we would argue, is the exact antithesis of the way our culture handles relationships. If we were rewriting this story to mirror the world's perspective on the Right Way, the servant would have walked up to the well, declared he was looking for a wife for Isaac, set up a table, and begun taking interviews. When Rebekah showed up, she may or may not have chosen to be who she really was because she would have wanted to be who she thought he wanted her to be. Or for a different modern scenario: The servant, Rebekah, and Isaac are all at a party. The servant tells Rebekah that Isaac is interested in her and then makes a quick exit. Isaac comes up, asks Rebekah to dance, they size each other up, dance, and try to act in a way that will lead to a date. Later they might talk. The whole process of "finding someone" degenerates into a kick-the-tires test that relies on emotion and attraction more than on building a relationship with another human being.

Our culture's tendency in relating to the opposite sex could be summed up in the following progression:

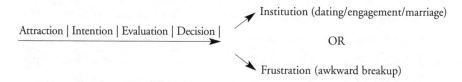

At the beginning of this progression, we communicate intention to the person we are attracted to before we evaluate what our obligation in doing so should be. This is how people get hurt, because our communication ends up overstating our level of commitment. If we determine we're not as much of a match with the other person as we once thought we were, we have nowhere to go but apart, despite all that has been invested in the relationship. John Stone, an assistant coordinator of Reformed University Fellowship and general dating guru, bluntly puts it this way when couples get to that stage and ask him for his counsel: "Get married or break up." Those are the only two choices. Because there is no middle ground, the relationship usually ends in like or loathing, and this is when, to quote the classic, heartfelt refrain of the J. Geils Band, "Love stinks."

Here is a different progression to consider:

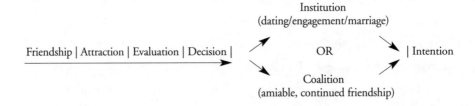

By starting with friendship and then rearranging the last four components of the equation (attraction, evaluation, decision, and intention), we create a much healthier way to think about a future significant other. By deciding what we think about another person *in his or her current context* and *before* we communicate any kind of intention toward him or her, we keep ourselves from communicating something that we're not ready to back up with a long-term commitment. We create a system and a mind-set much more dependent upon the sovereignty of God to open doors with the other person in his time—not necessarily in our own.

The Right Way is the way of honesty, integrity, faithfulness, purity, and accountability.[7] Vulnerability is important in appropriate amounts—even when the desire for relationship has been evaluated, decided, and communicated. It's important to make sure you are progressing in your relationship at a reasonable rate, protecting your heart from revealing too much too soon.

Proverbs 4:23 says, "Above all else, guard your heart, for it is the wellspring of life." Many couples go too far too fast both physically and emotionally. Many look at wedding rings before they've had their first real fight. They pick out china patterns before they really know each other. If they eventually do break up, those activities make parting all the more painful and confusing.

You need to talk at a level appropriate to your commitment, which means

---

7. For instance, I (Doug) realized that after 11 P.M. I started to get tired and would make worse and worse decisions. So Julie and I decided not to be together after eleven o'clock. We sometimes failed, but my realizing a point of weakness and taking steps ahead of time to alleviate possibilities for impurity helped immensely.

that there are some things about yourself you shouldn't share until you're with the person you absolutely know you're going to marry; some things should be reserved for him or her alone.

The Right Time

The last of the three "Rights" is the Right Time. Are you ready to be married? None of us is really *ever* ready, but we can ask, Does it make sense to be married now? Maybe—or maybe not. Do you have some goals that are best accomplished while you're still single? Are you prepared to accept the financial responsibility of being married? Do others around you affirm and encourage your relationship? Are you willing to wait any longer? Can you see any positive trade-offs that might come with postponing your wedding? Do you realize there is a very real possibility that despite birth control you could get pregnant on your honeymoon?[8] Are you ready for that?

Before I (Craig) met Megan, I was seriously involved with a girl named Heather at Mizzou. We had been together for only eleven months with two years of college still left for both of us, so you might think the idea of marriage would have seemed a bit premature to us. But it didn't—we thought we were in love. In our minds it was only a matter of time before we tied the knot, graduated, made babies, and lived happily ever after.

Well, it *was* only a matter of time for something to happen. Heather took a semester off, moved to South Carolina, met someone else, and broke up with me. Her words on that strange long-distance phone call: "I can't do this anymore." I couldn't either. The timing (not to mention the geography of it all) wasn't right and neither of us was willing or able to make the kind of commitment we had talked and thought about so much. We were young in every way you could imagine. I don't blame her. I just thank God for keeping us from making a huge mistake and, instead, working out good through our circumstances.

Now don't read a legalistic warning into this story. There's no magical, perfect time to get married. Delightful marriages have begun when the bride

---

8. For more on this, talk to Doug.

and groom were both eighteen, and other happily married couples didn't even meet until they were thirty-eight. You have to be content with the plan and timetable that our sovereign and good God has for you, but often that isn't something you can easily discern. God's calendar may not be yours. You may have always imagined yourself as married at twenty-seven, but you may find the Right Person at twenty-three. Or you may pass twenty-seven and hit thirty-three, still single. Being okay with God's plan and desiring to do things on his timetable shows maturity, although it can be difficult to adjust our plans of how we thought our lives would go. Just make sure that if you're heading toward marriage you can answer with some stability why you're ready *now* to make the commitments necessary to have a great marriage.

One last thought on this idea of the Right Time. In the book of Ruth, the marriage of Ruth to Boaz was because of love, but it was also for another reason at a significant time in Israel's history; namely, that Boaz's new land acquisition through marriage would be maintained. Love and vision, both wrapped in a sovereign timeliness, eventually led to the birth of the child Obed, who was the father of Jesse, who was the father of David...all the way to Jesus (Ruth 4:21-22).

The point? While probably the most significant human relationship we will ever have, marriage is still subject to the larger kingdom of God. It's important to talk long and hard about what kingdom purposes you have as a couple and if there's a Right Time to see them come to fruition. If you and your significant other can't answer some of these questions, the Right Person in the Right Way might not really matter—it just may not be the Right Time.

Love and R-E-S-P-E-C-T

So you've found the Right Person, you're relating to each other in the Right Way, and all signs seem to point to the fact that it's the Right Time. What now? In Ephesians 5 we find the most extensive passage in the Bible regarding marriage, so it would seem important to take a look at what our job descriptions should be if we indeed take the marriage plunge.

Listen to Ephesians 5:21: "Submit to one another out of reverence for

Christ." Such a simple verse with such profound implications. Our "reverence for Christ" means that we are awed before the reality of Christ, we are completely abandoned to him. This allows us to serve other people instead of ourselves. Paul tells us that we must be humble, we must die to self, and we must not let selfishness rule us. There's no way to live that sort of life, especially in the close confines of marriage, without the gospel of grace and the Holy Spirit's working in our lives. But with that gospel, we have new power to love each other.

I (Doug) never realized how selfish I was until I got married. All of a sudden I had a roommate who was around all the time. She was there at night, in the morning, in the bathroom, in the kitchen, in the garage...everywhere. Of course, that was great much of the time—but not when she said she didn't like my eating dinner while watching *SportsCenter* or piling up the dishes until they grew legs and walked off or putting only one dollar's worth of gas in the car at a time. What was *her* problem?

Her problem was...me. It took a long time for me to come to grips with the fact that I no longer ruled my world but was now part of a team working together under the lordship of our Savior. The gospel should have led me to be a servant right away, but I hadn't thought about how that call to servanthood would manifest itself in my marriage.

So often we think of servanthood as going to Africa to help starving children. In fact, servanthood takes place most of the time right in our homes with our families and spouses and children. Do we die to self there? Probably not as much as we'd like to think. When we consider what Jesus has done for us, we are both strengthened and humbled by the "gospel self-esteem" that allows us to repent of our weaknesses and serve in the strength of Christ.

This is where the rest of Ephesians 5 comes into play. In verses 22-30 Paul gives specific instructions to both men and women as to how they are to relate to one another, summing up his directives in verse 33: "Each one of you [husbands] also must love his wife as he loves himself, and the wife must respect her husband."

We don't want to oversimplify the nuances of marriage, but it seems the heart and art of marriage really boils down to two things: love and respect. It's interesting, though, that while both directives certainly apply to husband and wife, Paul makes a point to assign one predominantly to each: husband—love your wife; wife—respect your husband.

It's essential for both the husband and the wife to love and respect each other, but Paul's specific instructions point out our inherent weaknesses as men and women—the places where we need Jesus the most. For example, it's not too difficult for me (Craig) to find ways to respect Megan. She's a great mother to our kids, is talented and creative in all she does, and is wholeheartedly committed to follow me as I try to follow God. The bigger challenge for me sometimes is to *love* her, to relate to her with my whole person. Respect comes easier to me. Loving her means not always trying to fix her or make sense of her emotions. That can be more difficult.

Likewise, while there are plenty of things Megan loves about me, her test is to respect me even when I make bad decisions or lash out at the kids or struggle with work. Even though she loves me, Megan could be tempted to point to my failures as reasons to make her own decisions and to forget about what I think. But Paul calls her in her role as my wife to respect me—even when I seem unrespectable at times—and hold me in high regard despite my numerous shortcomings.

God knew what we needed when he offered these distinct instructions. Love, in particular, frees women to respect others and obey God. Respect, in particular, strengthens men to lead and love humbly.

Now even if any of this were easy in the first place, here's the catch: You can't *make* your spouse get his or her act together. Men, don't force your wife to respect you; love her in a new way, according to the gospel in your life. Women, don't harangue your husband to love you; respect him in a new way, according to the gospel in your life. As we bless each other in this way, we'll see true transformation in our own hearts first, and then in our marriages.

All this makes sense if you pause to think about it, but it's difficult to work out on a daily basis and nearly impossible to do without a hefty amount of grace and forgiveness. When it does happen it's beautiful, and probably the very thing that prompted these words in Proverbs 30:18-19:

There are three things that are too amazing for me,
>   four that I do not understand:
the way of an eagle in the sky,
>   the way of a snake on a rock,
the way of a ship on the high seas,
>   and the way of a man with a maiden.

For better or for worse, our marriage will usually set the tone for our lives. It has the power to influence us for good or for bad, no matter what is happening in the rest of our lives. If the world around us is crumbling but our marriage is strong and stable, then we move out into the world from a position of strength. If the world around us is great and successful but our marriage is crumbling and breaking, we move out into the world from a position of weakness. This is why marriage—and Ephesians 5—is so important.

And Now a Word from Our Hormones

The idea of marriage is great and wonderful, something to look forward to and pray about. It may afford us a best friend, someone to laugh with, cry with, pray with, wander with, and get naked with (Woo woo!). But how do we ensure that if we're married, sex stays within the context of marriage, or if we're single, that sex doesn't enter into our relationships or consume our thought life?

For starters, it's helpful to understand that despite what our culture (and sometimes our body) tells us, sex—unlike oxygen—is not an essential requirement for life. God has actually given the *gift* of singleness to some, made clear in the words of Paul (in 1 Corinthians 7) and even Jesus (in Matthew 19). Not having sex will not kill us.

But what if you don't have that particular gift of singleness or find that you lack self-control in this area? What do you do then? Paul mentions in the same 1 Corinthians 7 passage that if you feel as if you'll go crazy without sex, well, then, get married. You may say that's easier said than done! In reality, though God calls most of us to marry eventually, the problem is that a lot of us don't get married *when* we want to. Wondering if you're called to single-hood isn't very helpful when the fact remains that until you get married, you're called to singlehood. The issue then is contentment. Are you content to wait for God's timing, whatever it may turn out to be? Are you working too hard to try to get married, or are you working too hard at resisting the idea of marriage because of what you might have to give up?

Regardless of whether we are single or married, we need to seek healthy friendships with men and women, resisting the urge to "sexify" everything or to always view people as possible romances. We should get to know people for who they are and feel the freedom to simply be friends. If men and women can't be friends because the sex thing is always out there, our personal growth and connection as humans will be severely debilitated.[9]

Now we're not saying you'll never be attracted to someone once you become friends, nor should you be naive in your dealings with the opposite sex. But we do have to learn to be attracted to someone as a *person* and not just as an *object of desire.* True friendship can come from this and translate into mutual appreciation for the similarities between men and women as well as our differences.[10]

Another way to deal with the sexual tension is to try to erase some of the improper ideas and images that you've accumulated growing up. You can work on this by having intentional friendships with those of the opposite gender, but some of these issues won't come up until you're dating someone.

For instance, one of the most common dating questions is, How far is too far physically? That question says a lot in itself because it assumes that approaching sex but falling just short of it does not have any repercussions. We

---

9. For a two-hour treatment of this discussion, rent the 1989 flick *When Harry Met Sally.*

10. In this same vein, read both *Reviving Ophelia* by Mary Pipher (New York: Ballantine, 2002) and *Raising Cain* by Dan Kindlon and Michael Thompson (New York: Ballantine, 2000). Read the first book to better understand your own experience, and read the other to gain a glimpse at what your male or female friends may go through. Talk about these books with friends at an appropriate level and be sensitive to what you're learning about the other side.

should instead ask, What can I do to glorify God and respect this other person? Or simply, How pure can we be?[11]

Whether or not we're dating, becoming more pure might mean being more careful with what our minds take in on a daily basis. Television ads, direct mail, the Internet, movies, and even the most bland television channels put things in front of our eyes that we shouldn't be looking at. Job 31:1 says, "I made a covenant with my eyes not to look lustfully at a girl." That's a good start, since we can make choices to avoid certain magazines or Internet sites or movies. We need to ask, What is true and lovely? What is right? What expresses truth about the world, and what is a lie?

We need purity not only of the eyes but also of the heart. Worse than the images we see are the messages associated with them: You have to have unmarried sex to be happy; you need to look like a supermodel to be popular; you will fulfill your deepest longings if you succumb to your sinful desires. Standing up against temptation is not a popular prime-time topic. C. S. Lewis writes,

> Only those who try to resist temptation know how strong it is…that is why bad people know very little about badness. They have lived a sheltered life by always giving in. We never find out the strength of the evil impulse inside us until we fight it: and Christ, because He was the only Man who never yielded to temptation, is also the Man Who knows to the full what temptation means—the only complete realist.[12]

First Corinthians 10:13 says that God will give us the ability to withstand any temptation, even though resisting it will sometimes make us look like complete fools in the world's eyes.

Our friend Matt lived a wild lifestyle in high school and the early part of college. When he came to faith in Christ, he began trying to live out his new identity by fleeing from any kind of temptation that presented itself. He memorized 2 Timothy 2:22, which starts off, "Flee the evil desires of youth."

---

11. Please, though, seek to be pure without being puritanical. Never looking at or talking to members of the opposite sex would be a bad application of this idea.
12. C. S. Lewis, *Mere Christianity* (San Francisco: Harper, 1952), 142.

One night Matt got a ride home from class from a married woman. At a stoplight she leaned over and put her hand on his knee. The verse flashed through his mind. He responded quite literally by jumping out of the car and leaving the woman at the intersection as he ran the rest of the way home. Now that's application![13]

But what if we've blown it? What if Matt hadn't jumped out of the car, and they ended up driving to a motel somewhere with one thing leading to another? Yikes. Then what? Second Corinthians 7:10 says, "Godly sorrow brings repentance that leads to salvation and leaves no regret, but worldly sorrow brings death." If you are truly sorry for the injury you have caused others, yourself, and Christ, then you should cry out to God for forgiveness and run back to him like the prodigal son. Remember what happened when the son decided to return to his father? "While he was still a long way off, his father saw him and was filled with compassion for him; he ran to his son, threw his arms around him and kissed him" (Luke 15:20).

A friend of mine (Doug's) recently told me he was falling in love with a woman. He told me that she didn't have a pure past, and it was something she was ashamed of. They hadn't talked about it yet, but he wondered how he should handle that conversation.

He and I talked about how we are all sexually broken. Every one of us. Even though he hadn't sinned in the particular ways she had, and even though her sins might have had different consequences, he couldn't relate to her as a pure man to a broken sinner. They were both broken sinners. He had the chance to illustrate the gospel for her when they talked about their need for forgiveness and reconciliation.

We all need to hear that message. Our impurities will haunt and eventually destroy us if we keep them hidden. God asks us to repent and cry out to him to save us. We must be honest with others and seek counsel and prayer as we begin the road to healing.

When it comes to living a life of purity in the face of temptation, we have

---

13. I (Doug) reacted much the same way one night at college when a girl kept scooting closer and closer to me until she was playing with my leg hair.

to have the courage to choose a different lifestyle, a lifestyle that doesn't just say no to the desires of youth but fills that void with something. Second Timothy 2:22 goes on to say, "pursue righteousness, faith, love and peace, along with those who call on the Lord out of a pure heart." So many times we meet Christians who think life is a series of don'ts. As much as we need to run *from* temptation, we need to run *to* purity, *to* righteousness, *to* Christ and his satisfaction. Thus we flee *from* something *to* something. Hear the words of Augustine: "A temptation has sprung up; it is the wind; thou art disturbed; it is a wave. Awake up Christ then, let Him speak with thee. 'Who is this, since the winds and the sea obey Him?'"

We should pursue godliness in our sexual lives because Christ loves us and wants the best for us. He promises life for us. As Augustine said, when we are tempted either to love evil or to think of ourselves as righteous, it's time to awaken Christ and let him speak.

"Who Am I?" Times Two

So there you have it—our thoughts on love. Who would have imagined two guys from the Midwest could have summed up the subtleties of this complicated topic in one simple chapter? Truth be told, we're not all that romantic (just ask Megan and Julie—ah, the stories they *couldn't* tell). We're still in the process of learning about who we are as we evaluate how we respond to the commitment love requires. At times in our lives, we've been up to the task of serving, caring, and loving, and that has been its own wonderful reward. At other times we've wrestled with our commitment to love, and that has been harder than we could have imagined.

But looking back through the sagas of our own romantic pursuits, we're thankful that we had mentors to show us some truths about relating to the opposite sex. We learned from them that how we think about our significant other is crucial to the success of our marriage. Our application of love and respect begins long before we say "I do." But it certainly doesn't end at the altar.

If we find ourselves called to marriage, if we search for the Right Person in the Right Way at the Right Time, all the while keeping our hormones in check, we might end up with a tremendous opportunity to answer the who-am-I question with another human being. It should excite us (not to mention scare the living stuffing out of us) to realize that we can help someone we care very much about to answer this same important question.

Ideas of Things to Do

If You're Single

- Don't buy into the cultural standards of what makes a worthy mate. Take the time to discover what God says makes a worthy mate. Discuss these with your friends.

- If you choose to date, don't seriously date someone you wouldn't marry.

- Go out and have fun with people. Initiate friendships.

- Remember that it's okay for a man and woman to go out and have dinner without its being a huge deal, but be wise the second and third time. Eventually it can become a big deal.

- Spend a lot of time with same-sex friends talking about the issues presented in this chapter. Be real and honest about your struggles, and get some help and accountability for the issues you're dealing with.

- Memorize 1 Corinthians 10:13 and take it seriously.

- Don't have sex until you're married. If you already have, ask God for forgiveness and resolve from that point on to save sex for your husband or your wife.

- Don't think that marriage will provide all the answers to your problems. Marriage is hard and so often only magnifies the issues you're already struggling with. Get to know some married couples and ask them to be honest and vulnerable about how marriage is for them.

- Don't just try to find the Right Person for you; try to be the Right Person for someone else.

- Keep asking that who-am-I question as you think about dating or getting married. Otherwise you might get wrapped up in the circumstances or the conquest and try to answer the What-will-I-do? question by getting married before you're ready.

If You're Engaged

- Make sure you get some good marriage counseling and start applying it plenty of time ahead. This is a chance to talk some things out and get further understanding about marriage with good biblical foundations. (You may even want to go for preengagement counseling!)
- Try not to be engaged for more than eight or nine months. If you think you should be engaged for longer than a year, why not just wait and get engaged a bit later? The longer the engagement, the more temptation lies ahead, not to mention the headache of spending more time than you need to plan the wedding.
- Don't live together until you're married.
- Try to enjoy being engaged. It's a very weird time since you're sort of in between everything, but it can be a time of great joy and expectation!
- Have a fun wedding. Remember that the goal is to get married, not to have a show-stopping wedding. Don't blow every penny you have on something that will last only a few hours and leave you destitute for the next ten years.
- Try not to go very far into debt for a honeymoon. Get advice from others who have gone before you. Have fun! The most important thing is not the location but the fact that you're now on a vacation with your new spouse! Hey, that even could be fun in Hays, Kansas, right?!
- Talk to your closest friends and even your pastor (and/or his wife) or a church counselor about sex on the wedding night. Realize that it's not exactly like it's pictured in the movies.

If You're Married

- Be intentional about setting up your house after you're married. This is a great time to figure out some priorities for where you'll live, how much stuff you'll have, etc.

- Get involved in a young marrieds class at your church or start one. Also, hang out with and ask questions of couples who have been married for ten, twenty-five, and even fifty years.
- Ask around about birth control. Get as much information as possible, and don't just assume certain things. Figure out what best expresses your understanding and convictions.
- Try to live off only one income so if and when you have kids and one of you stays home, you won't have that big of a financial adjustment to make.
- Make a commitment that marriage is for a lifetime. Never throw the word *divorce* around casually as a joke, threat, or consideration.
- Marriage is a cross-cultural experience. Take care to get to know the other person not only before you get married but also afterward. What type of toothpaste does she like? Does he like sleeping with the windows open or closed? How will you divide up household responsibilities such as the cooking and food shopping? What about decisions on moving? the number of kids? holidays? These can be areas of cross-cultural tension, but they can also be resolved somewhat easily if you talk about them.

Wherever You Are

- Limit or stop any media intake that isn't helping. Ask someone to hold you accountable to stop watching bad movies or pornography on the Internet. The lie is that it won't affect you, but it will—as well as those around you.
- Enjoy your friends. Get to know them. Delight in them.
- Talk to people who have been in the same situation you are. Ask them questions. Consider their advice. Sometimes that can make all the difference in realizing you are not alone.

CHAPTER TEN

Community

LIVING WITH ALL KINDS OF FOLKS

*Men are mirrors, or "carriers" of Christ to other men. Sometimes
unconscious carriers. This "good infection" can be carried by those who have
not got it themselves. People who were not Christians themselves helped me
to Christianity. But usually it is those who know Him that bring Him to
others. That is why the Church, the whole body of Christians showing Him
to one another, is so important. You might say that when two Christians
are following Christ together there is not twice as much Christianity as
when they are apart, but sixteen times as much.*

—C. S. LEWIS, *Mere Christianity*

He ain't heavy, he's my brother.

—THE HOLLIES

A hundred years ago some people barely traveled more than a few miles
from their homes. If traveling was an option, the whole family usually
traveled together, and it had to be for a very good reason. Back then, home
was where you hung your hat, and the hat hook rarely moved.

Today, however, most of us will move at least six to seven times during our
lifetimes—from neighborhood to neighborhood, city to city, state to state, or
even country to country. While our grandparents may have stayed at the same
job for a lifetime, today it is rare to find someone who has been in the same
office for five years. We float between churches and get involved in small
groups designed to meet for only a period of weeks rather than months.

We experience fragmentation and change particularly in our twenties. Our friends get married and move away; we get married and our spouse gets a job transfer; we change jobs as we try to find a career fit; we struggle to get involved in a church that seems to have different people attending every week. We get so busy meeting people that we rarely take time to get real and actually know them. We sometimes want the process of knowing and being known to be microwavable and come out in a matter of a few weeks. Then, in the back of our minds, we wonder if it's worth it, since they or we will probably move on to somewhere else in a few years anyway. Why bother?

This transitory and disjointed way of living causes us to miss out on the relationships that can come only after an accumulation of years and experiences together. Long-term connections are such a strange notion today that we've lost a sense of rootedness, a connection to the place and people of our past that speaks to a deeper part of who we are. We've lost a sense of community. As the decade of our twenties feeds into our moving, on-the-go culture, a couple of nagging questions remain: Is there something more, and does anyone else care?

Yes. God created us to need community. We are not just individuals; we are a people joined together by family, church, and living life together. We may live in the woods of Montana or in downtown Boston, but we're in this together. That's why that longing, those nagging questions, won't go away. God didn't intend them to.

As we continue looking at the who-am-I question, we need to look into how our relationships shape and mold us. Chances are we will learn an awful lot about ourselves as we learn more about those around us, why we need them, and why they need us.

The Power of the Practice of Community

A couple years ago I (Doug) had an opportunity to think about this concept of connection firsthand. After I graduated from seminary in St. Louis and before we moved to Norman, Oklahoma, Julie, the kids, and I lived in the basement of my parents' home for five months. There I was—thirty, married, three small children—in my parents' basement in Ozark, Missouri. Honestly, I had hoped to achieve a little higher status for myself by this stage in my life.

But God used that time to reconnect me with my family and my past. My kids saw their grandparents every day for five months, my parents saw their grandchildren change every day as they grew in their knowledge and experiences, and I got to watch the whole thing happen. I marveled at what was taking place—connection—before my very eyes.[1]

In addition to the extra time with my folks, I reconnected with my hometown. I took drives to many of my favorite high-school hangouts and thought about how my life had changed since I'd last been there. I played basketball on Sunday nights with guys I had grown up with, and we exchanged jokes and stories that were fifteen to twenty years old. This past—a history that I had been denying and had in many ways rejected—is now much more a part of me. While I'm glad to be where I am now, leaving my good old hometown hit me harder than I would have thought.

The early church seemed to understand its need for connection better than we do today. That shouldn't surprise us, especially in light of the shock of Jesus' crucifixion and resurrection. Such shared experience is not something from which they could just walk away, pretending it had never happened. They needed one another to make sense of it and reflect on it.

In Acts 2 we read about how that group of Christians was trying to understand the challenges and changes that came with their faith in Jesus. They determined that being *together* in every way possible was the best and most important thing they could do, and they felt the strong need to connect with one another as they began their new lives.

And so they did. Acts says they gathered together to learn, to talk, to pray, to worship. They saw many great things that left them with a sense of wonder and awe about what they believed. They sold their possessions and gave to others who were in need.[2] They met corporately—formally and informally—

---

1. I also got to play racquetball and watch *Junkyard Wars* with my dad.
2. Don't be misled here—this wasn't the official beginning of communism. Communism says, "What's yours is mine." Christianity, on the other hand, says, "What's mine is yours." There's a big difference.

"with glad and sincere hearts, praising God and enjoying the favor of all the people" (Acts 2:46-47). Their commitment to community not only had a powerful effect on the members of the group, but it garnered favor from those around them, and they saw God add more and more people to their number. This togetherness was the key to the early church's growth as well as the growth of the kingdom of God.

An interesting note: We've already mentioned Genesis 11 and the Tower of Babel. The Scriptures record that this time "the whole world had one language and a common speech" (Genesis 11:1), and God was concerned about this arrogant use of unity: "If as one people speaking the same language they have begun to do this, then nothing they plan to do will be impossible for them" (verse 6). Thus the Trinity confused their language so they would not understand one another and be able to build the tower for their own posterity. The point here? If God himself said, "If as one people...they...do this,...nothing...will be impossible for them," think about the potential power of *real* community for good or evil. Acts 2, in a sense, is the reversal of the Tower of Babel. In the gospel the nations come together again, and we see the restoration of community as God intended.

Community should not be taken for granted, either in its presence or in its potential, because of the way the collective group can influence the individual. Let's look more specifically at some different areas of community in which we need to be actively involved in our twenties.

Family: Relating to the Relatives

"Honor your father and your mother, so that you may live long in the land the LORD your God is giving you" (Exodus 20:12). Most of us are familiar with these words. But what do they mean in real life in our twenties?

God says that our human relationships are a reflection of our relationship to him—a relationship of loving authority. He establishes governments, officials, pastors, elders, and parents to have authority over us. But the family is the backbone for these other structures. Our societies are built on families. This is one reason why, in the theocracy of Israel, God took great pains to protect the family. Whenever there was trouble within the family, it became a communal issue. Threats to the family were seen as threats to the whole nation and were dealt with seriously.[3]

Some of you grew up in great families. Rejoice. God has given you a great inheritance. Others of you, however, grew up in families that hurt you deeply. Thinking of God as Father may be difficult. You may have been wounded in your understanding of what it means to be loved, to be vulnerable, to be cared for. All of the good and bad in your background will influence how you relate to your family in your twenties and how you honor your parents through a time of great changes in relating to them.

When you went away to college or moved away from home to work, you entered a serious stage of transition. That was an important time in your relationship with your parents, and in some ways that transition is still going on. You may or may not talk about it much with them, but your parents probably still struggle with how to relate to you, wonder about the amount of respect and distance you wish to have, and remember you as the sweet little tyke running around the house only twenty or so years ago.

Finding that right balance of new relating isn't easy. Some people never do move away from home but remain in the same relationship structure in which they've grown up. Others make the perfunctory Mother's Day and Father's Day phone calls and visit now and then, but they emotionally detach from their families once they're out and have moved on.

Though it isn't always convenient or perhaps even pleasant, we should resist the extremes of enmeshment and abandonment and seek to connect or reconnect with our families in healthy ways. For whatever reason, God has

---

3. To put it positively: "And insofar as all authority which men possess comes from him, he speaks according to the legitimate civil order, which means that if we are careful to render him the homage which he is due, if each in his own place obeys those who are in authority over him, if each takes into account his own estate and condition, if children honor their fathers and mothers, if everyone honors those who sit in the seat of justice, and servants do the same towards their masters, in brief, there will be a beautiful harmony among us for our peace, according to the order which our Lord has established, which is to be held inviolable by us." (John Calvin, *Sermons on the Ten Commandments,* ed. Benjamin W. Farley [Grand Rapids: Baker, 1980], 137.)

placed them in our lives to give us our particular story. It may be a sad story or a grand one, but either way, we need to make sense of it to the extent we can. We need to embrace it or even redeem it if need be.

I (Craig) went through quite a transition with my family in my twenties—mostly good, but not without some speed bumps. It probably didn't help that my parents and I got off to a rocky start when they dropped me off at college, and Mom, while making my bed for the first (and last) time in McDavid dorm, said something to the effect of, "So when do you think you'll be home?" Being the overly eager college freshman who had waited for this moment since he was sixteen, I said, "Mom, this *is* home." Not exactly the best way to include the family in the midst of my first major transition.

But that was just the beginning. Over the years my parents and I had some tough discussions about which major I would pursue, why I planned to pack up and move to Colorado after graduation, and how I was planning to repay college loans while raising my own financial support. Several years later, after Megan and I began dating, got engaged, got married, and eventually had kids, the topics of conversation ranged from who this new person in my life was to when the kids might get some time with their grandparents to how many toys were just too many at Christmas.

None of these topics was out of line. My tone in the midst of them, however, was probably uncalled for at times. Looking back, I realize that I perhaps overreacted toward my parents because I was so overwhelmed with the flood of new experiences and ideas that were coming at me all at once. And as I was trying to figure out who I was—son? missionary? fiancé? husband? dad? Scrooge?—in the midst of all these new situations, my parents were also trying to determine what *their* new roles were—parents? financial supporters? empty nesters? in-laws? grandparents? Santa?

Thankfully, despite the inundation of life and my own occasional melancholic pessimism about it, my relationship with my parents grew because we chose to process our experiences together, always honestly and sometimes painfully. We may not have understood one another all the time, but we cared for one another and were intentional about strengthening our relationship in the midst of all the changes. As a result, we grew in our comprehension of what God was doing not only in me as I grew more confident in who I was becoming but also in them as they graciously let go of me to be the person they raised me to be. We're still doing this as our lives and relationships continue to change.

The decade of our twenties is a good time to answer the who-am-I question in light of our family because not only are *we* pursuing new ideas at a new stage of life, but our parents, siblings, and even extended family have probably changed and developed over the years. Odds are that as much as you want them to see your personal evolution take place, they want you to see theirs as well, and it takes time and being together for that to happen.

If you had trouble at home, and getting out of the house was a tremendous relief, look for ways to forgive and restore your family relationships.[4] If your parents are divorced, have you truly dealt with that? Have you talked with someone, perhaps a counselor, about this and how it has affected you? Do you blame yourself? These types of questions need to be asked and answered, or the process of dealing with them will continue into your thirties and beyond, possibly affecting your spouse and kids.

A good friend of mine grew up in a pretty messed-up home. Derek, the youngest of three, grew up in Indiana, saw his parents divorce and his dad leave when he was young, and his whole family fall apart afterward. In the wake of the chaos, Derek decided that if anything good was going to happen in his life, it was up to him to make it so. Though he lived with his mom, he was basically on his own from age thirteen on, partying through high school and living out the lyrics of most of the songs written at the time by fellow Indianan John Mellencamp.[5]

After graduating from high school, Derek became a Christian on a cross-country bike trip. He started his own construction company in college, renovating old houses for Indiana University and putting himself through school in the process. He now is on staff with The Navigators in Colorado Springs.

---

4. If you look at the patriarchs of the Bible, you will see serious family dysfunction. Yet God worked through each of those families to bring about his divine purposes.

5. Specifically, "Hurts So Good," "Jack and Diane," "Pink Houses," "Lonely Ol' Night," "Small Town," and "Authority Song" from Mellencamp's greatest-hits album, *The Best That I Could Do (1978–1988)*.

Because of the dysfunction in their families, Derek and his wife, Angie (who also comes from a divorced home), and their two children have the world's worst holiday travel schedule. They try to see as many of the multiple sides of their families as they can. In addition, Derek has initiated a relationship with his father, a well-paid business consultant, and makes an effort to see him at least once a year, despite his father's unpredictable travel schedule.

In every conversation we've had about his family, I've never heard Derek speak bitterly about his father or his past. In fact, Derek and Angie consider themselves the first generation to end the cycle of dysfunction in their families and set a new foundation for their kids. They have not run, hidden, or felt sorry for themselves about their situation, but instead they have resolved to address it head on, deal with the awkwardness of it all, and not give up on their family relationships, strained though they may be.

You may identify with Derek, or you may be in another place, perhaps *too* dependent on your parents. If you're in that situation, you may need to consider why you've been so reliant on them. Do your parents hold too much sway in your decisions? Whether you live next door to your parents or in a different state, you may not have left home emotionally. That fact often comes to light when you get married, but it can be unhealthy before then as well. You may need to go ahead and ask your parents for their advice, but try to do a few more things on your own.

Some of you may still be living with your parents as Doug was. For your sake (as well as your folks), we hope this is only a temporary situation. Establishing your own place is an important aspect of your twenties. Sure, risk taking doesn't always work out, and it's nice to have the option of temporarily moving back home if things go awry, but living on your own away from "your room"[6] is an important transition. Don't just play the no-money card and move back in with your folks for too long. Figure it out as soon as you can.

Finally, if you've been a brat, it might be a good time for you to consider

---

6. Which will probably be turned into a guest room. I (Craig) hadn't been at college a full semester when my folks turned my room into a den. Looking back, this wasn't that big a deal, but the speed with which that decision was made was a bit disturbing when it happened.

the sacrifices your parents have made and the hardships they have gone through to get you to this point and start asking more questions to get to know them again. Many of us revert back to our sixteen-year-old personas—messy, whiny, selfish—when we go home for a visit. Relating in new ways with our brothers, sisters, and parents takes time and requires new habits. It's important that we strive to make the effort to do this because our families need to see that our character is changing, and we need to acknowledge that our family is changing as well.

In all these things, as you continue to forge ahead into adulthood, remember that you are pursuing Christlikeness in all of life—and your family is included in that all-of-life category. Consider how you can serve them and love them and treat them with respect and honor, because you'll need to deal with your parents (and brothers and sisters, too) in this different way for quite some time.

Friends: Keeping the Connections

Our friends influence us more than we can imagine. First Corinthians 15:33 says, "Do not be misled: 'Bad company corrupts good character.' " Regardless of our age or experience, who we're around will affect who we turn out to be. Why? A community of like-minded people helps us flesh out our faith and what it means.

We remember the fascinating surprise of going to college and finding hundreds and thousands of other people in the exact same stage of life as we were. So many choices of involvement and interaction—the Rugby Club, the Save the Grass Society, Students Against Students Against Things, etc. Our participation in or with any of these groups meant new friends, ideas, and influences. And that was rather cool.

Now, in our postcollegiate days, we still have some ability to pick our friends, but as we get older we're thrown into more situations where—for better or for worse—they seem to get picked for us. We don't get to choose our next-door neighbors or our coworkers, and yet we still have to figure out how to make all these relationships work. Sure, we still can join groups and societies along our lines of particular interest, but since we have so much less disposable time, we may not get out quite as much as we once did.

As if figuring out our current context isn't complex enough, maintaining relationships with our past circles of buddies can be downright hard. Moving again and again affords us opportunities to find new friends but severs ties with others at the same time.

Maybe you couldn't *wait* to choose new friends when you moved, or maybe you're still searching the Internet to find the best friend you've lost touch with. We need a healthy perspective here. You've probably realized that it's not realistic to think that all of those high-school and college friendships will last forever. Geography and time work against us, and sometimes we need to get to a point of remembering a relationship, being thankful for it, and letting go without feeling guilty that it's just not working. It's not the other person's fault that the friendship is not as it was, and it's not our fault, either. We entered a season together and enjoyed it, but the time comes when we must exit from it as well.

Even if we have only a few close friends, we still have to work at those relationships. If we get cynical or lazy about those friendships, we stunt our own growth in discovering who we are because we've stopped taking the time to know who our friends are in the context of community. As Dr. Donald Guthrie says, "The cynical nature of our culture permeates the lives of people around me—and me. And only community can stand against that. We discover who we are—and who we are meant to be—face to face and side by side with others in work, love and learning."[7] You can see your flaws and strengths when someone who knows and loves you walks with you along the way.

My (Doug's) closest friendships today are the ones I formed in my early twenties. What started with ski trips, "We're-Number-One!" chants, grooming our mullets, early morning Bible study discussions, and talking about girls has progressed to marriages and kids, seminary and careers, highlights and

---

7. Dr. Donald Guthrie, quoted in Steven Garber, *The Fabric of Faithfulness* (Downers Grove, Ill.: InterVarsity, 1997), 147.

heartaches. Most of us try to get together at least once a year to reconnect, and I have a dream that we could all live in the same community someday.

As you approach your next change or reevaluate where you're at in life, think about who you want to spend time with, and then strive to connect with those people. Friendship won't always happen right away, but it will never happen if you keep to yourself just wishing it would. In the same way, if you are already in a great group, reach out to others who are looking for the same thing. This keeps you from getting lazy in relating to new people, and it may also meet someone else's need for community. When you grab someone new and take him or her along, you will likely earn gratefulness forever and may enter into a new friendship that just might last a lifetime.

Church: The Body, Not the Building

While we won't be able to exhaustively cover here the full doctrine of the church, we do hope to offer some insights into how church can help us answer the who-am-I question as it relates to community.

Many twentysomethings struggle with finding their place in church. Over time you may have moved from fellowship to fellowship and then perhaps to different groups within the same fellowship (youth group to college to singles to young marrieds to married with kids...) and still not found your niche. It doesn't take long before we start asking questions like, Where do I fit? Who do I connect with? And why does it matter anyway?

It matters because as Christians we've been called to and placed in the body of Christ. We can't deny this; the Bible says it. In addition to our family and our friends, the church is the main place for us to ascertain who we are while we continue to "spur one another on toward love and good deeds" (Hebrews 10:24). For these reasons the church should be filled with twenty-somethings serving humbly, learning, and leading in the body of Christ. But often in our twenties we abandon the church altogether or at best give it only token attendance.

We may have reasons for this lack of engagement. Perhaps we have been ignored by someone in the church or have been hurt by a church, its leadership, or its members. When you gather that many sinners together in one place, none of this should seem that surprising.

Some of the neglect may truly be the fault of the leadership to care for its people. But some of the blame probably lies with us and the condition of *our* hearts. And that is the only part we can begin to do something about. If we believe that the transitory aspect of our twenties excuses us from discovering more about ourselves by engaging with God's people, could a church leader get to know us even if he wanted to? Would we be humble, teachable, and faithful, or would we just have a list of reasons why we don't feel the need to connect?

The church history of my (Craig's) twenties is not a particularly exemplary one, due mostly to my unfair evaluation of churches and their pastors. There were the megachurch wannabes and the small corner churches and the legalistic churches and the anything-goes churches. While I knew there was no such thing as the perfect church, my preferences (which I called standards at the time) left me in the dark as to exactly what I was looking for; thus, churches and pastors passed like street signs in the headlights—most of them hard to read and none of them leading to where I thought I wanted to go.

I was relentless in my reasoning as to why I didn't really need church, falling into the trap of asking, What's in it for me? instead of, What's in it for God?[8] As a result, I probably missed out on some great opportunities to meet new people and grow together with them. The only answer this experience provided to Who am I? was that I was a judgmental church consumer who was preoccupied with his own inclinations and opinions. And that wasn't really an answer that could help me much in my twenties…or in life.

The concept of church can be one of the most difficult for us to grasp at this time in our lives, especially since most of our experiences up to this point have led us away from the idea of interdependence in our relationships.

---

8. Thank you, Scott Morton, for this important question concerning the purpose of our worship.

Because so much of our formative years are focused on getting out on our own, the idea of choosing to place ourselves within some larger institution seems foreign to our thinking. We may also have a tough time understanding and embracing our need for connection with the larger body of Christ because we don't consider that the people around us also need attention and care, possibly from us.

One unique feature of the church is its vision of all kinds of people worshiping together, taking vows together, confessing together. And yet our culture, age, and affinities sometimes work against us as we are divided up in ways that are purely organizational rather than relational.

Cutting across some of these generational and situational barriers may mean volunteering in Vacation Bible School to meet the three-year-olds in your church. Or hanging out with the youth group to get to know them and their parents. Or driving an elderly member to church. Or sitting next to someone you would never normally talk to. These activities help us dismiss the it's-all-about-me viewpoint and get our eyes on God and others who make up the church.

Our ideas about church need to be radically altered. More and more, pastors are standing up and using the Bible as their text while essentially preaching sermons of their own opinions. Topical sermons abound, most of which lead us not to Christ but to how to live a better life. This may sound good and even biblical, but it doesn't help us understand the Bible better, nor does it truly lead us to grace and repentance. Biblical, expository preaching through books or large passages of the Bible needs to return to our pulpits. We should long for this theological underpinning and then seek to apply those truths to our lives. We need to attend churches that have this mind-set and value: The Bible alone rules our worship and our understanding of life.[9]

We also need to view church worship as the time when we actually *get* to gather together to sing and give, to hear the very words of God read and

---

9. For the last five hundred years this has been known as the principle of *Sola Scriptura*.

explained to us, to pray and take the Lord's Supper in ways that we cannot do by ourselves. We would benefit from preparing ourselves for the time by getting enough sleep the night before, by familiarizing ourselves with the hymns and spiritual songs, and by thinking about worship before we actually go. Perhaps if we do these things, worship will begin to permeate our souls, and we'll long for more times when we can be together.

We should also expect to get involved and seek to get others involved. It's easy enough to show up for church like we would a football game, ready to be entertained, but that's not the kind of participation God is looking for. We've been blessed with our gifts—however many we may have and whatever they may be—for a reason. If we sit on our hands and withhold what we're gifted at doing, the gifts will not disappear, but they certainly will not get developed. Again, this limits our ability to understand what we're good at and keeps back blessings from those who need what we have to offer.

At some point we have to decide that God wants us in this imperfect group and jump into the life of the church with both feet—a life of submission, of service, of volunteering, of study, of repentance, of praise, and of joy. God may be calling us to patch up some of the weaknesses we've seen, or he may be asking us to endure them. Brian Habig and Les Newsom put it this way in their book *The Enduring Community:*

> The most fundamental definition of the Church is the covenantal
> bond that you have with the person sitting next to you in the pew.
> Therefore, at the heart of your responsibilities in the Church must be
> intentionality in building relationships with others in your congrega-
> tion. This is more than just starting a supper club with a few of those
> congregation members with whom you have the most in common.
> This means bringing even those with whom you would not naturally
> be inclined to relate into the fellowship of your home, your time, and
> your life.[10]

---

10. Brian Habig and Les Newsom, *The Enduring Community* (Jackson, Miss.: Reformed University Press, 2001), 178.

In other words, when we begin to ask the who-am-I question, we find we are a part of the kingdom of God—the body of believers and confessors that Christ came to seek and to save. We are connected to everyone else because we are *the building* (Ephesians 2:19-22), *the body* (Ephesians 4, 1 Corinthians 12), and *the bride* (Ephesians 5) of Christ. We're not independent of others; we need others in order to be healthy and fruitful. We've been called *out* and called *into* this new community, whose physical presence we can see only in the working of the local church. Our presence there is vital.

This is our hope: that twentysomethings would return to and reengage in the church, using their gifts and seeing true, grace-centered ministry take place as a result. The church is God's means for working through the world, and as we see throughout the Scriptures, he is serious about this work. We in our twenties need to join him in what he's doing, not only for the sake of the world, but also for the sake of our relationship with him.

The Case for Community

As it has been since the Garden of Eden, so it is now: We need others. We need community. God saw our need and met it, not with some spiritual salve or special word, but with another human being. And we've been reckless in our pursuit of relationships ever since.

Community calls us away from the myth that we can do all things by ourselves and invites us instead to experience the power of doing them with others. It calls us to slow down and dig in, to stop and even to stay. Community reminds us that even Jesus—Jesus!—never tried to go it alone but surrounded himself with others for companionship and encouragement. This is what community does, and this is what community is for—to keep us human, but not to let us just stay there either.

We need our families, as dysfunctional as they may be, to help us make sense of who we are. We need our friends to relive and create memories with us that keep us grounded. And we need those in the church—who are perhaps as desperate as we are—to help us grow as Christians and "make meaning" with us so we don't become narrow, flat, and static in our lives.

Parker Palmer puts it this way:

As I learn more about the seed of true self that was planted when I was born, I also learn about the ecosystem in which I was planted—the network of communal relations in which I was called to live responsively, accountably, and joyfully with beings of every sort. Only when I know both seed and system, self and community, can I embody the great commandment to love both my neighbor and myself.[11]

We need others, period. We always have and always will.

Ideas of Things to Do

- Take your mom or dad or both out to eat the next time you see them and thank them.
- Ask your grandparents to tell you stories about their childhoods.
- Forgive your parents and siblings if you need to, and don't forget to take responsibility for your part of the situation, making amends by asking them to forgive you.
- Go to a family reunion.
- Decide to start over if you had a family you weren't proud of (remember Derek's story).
- Call your parents regularly, not just on Mother's Day and Father's Day.
- Cultivate your friendships by making time, showing up, and asking questions.
- Go to church with the expectation of learning, growing, and giving, but also go with the expectation of meeting God there.
- Meet with the pastor and take him out for lunch or breakfast.
- Go to the various men's or women's retreats your church offers.

---

11. Parker Palmer, *Let Your Life Speak* (San Francisco: Jossey-Bass, 2000), 17.

- Start an adopt-a-college-student program at your church.
- Volunteer in the various outreach events and even plan some.
- Learn the old hymns and sing them from your heart.
- Learn to sing new songs, the hymns of today.
- Get to know people older and younger than you.
- Volunteer for nursery duty every once in a while. (Yikes!)

CHAPTER ELEVEN

Legacy

RETHINKING ACCOMPLISHMENT AND SUCCESS

We must learn that when the time comes that our pious works don't help and we find ourselves saying, I have done what I could; I have served my father and my master faithfully, I have defamed no one, and have not grumbled; I have faithfully instructed members of my household, my children, and employees; as far as possible I have ruled well; I have caused my neighbor no injury, nor have I stolen nor have I committed adultery. But to what avail? That will not help now. With all this the human heart will not be satisfied; it is frightened when it finds nothing which can stand before God Almighty and His judgment.

—MARTIN LUTHER

Be not anxious about what you have, but about what you are.

—GREGORY THE GREAT

Growing up in rural west central Illinois, I (Craig) spent a lot of time playing in cemeteries. Two hundred years earlier, life in middle America was harsh, and most rural churches were built with cemeteries surrounding them to bury those who died of old age, at birth, or from the elements. Two hundred years later church picnics and family reunions are held at little country churches that dot the plains. My family seemed to have more than its fair share of such gatherings, so I grew up very familiar with those small church graveyards.

I remember tossing water balloons, playing tag, and running all over the graves of people who had lived centuries before me while my parents and their friends talked for hours at a table covered with a red-checkered tablecloth and piled high with fried chicken and apple pies. Sometimes I stopped to read some of the weathered headstones in the cemetery, repeating the names of those buried beneath my feet and trying to imagine why they died. It was a fascinating part of my childhood; from a young age I began to think of death and come to grips with the fact that one day I, too, would die. As I look back on it now, those cemeteries were one reason I became a Christian. They got me thinking about my life, my death, and what lay beyond them both.[1]

These days we need more cemeteries in our suburbs. Think about it: When was the last time you drove by a cemetery in the middle of suburbia? In our culture we tend to hide death. We're forced to deal with it at funerals, but then we quickly climb back into our autopilot existence. We cringe at images of sick elderly people and hide them in convenient, out-of-the-main-stream nursing homes. We talk about death in an abstract sense when it happens somewhere else in the world or in our military past. Youth is all the rage in our television shows, movies, and music; immortality becomes the Holy Grail we're all after but can never find. Cemeteries in our suburbs would be an unwanted intrusion of death into a seemingly unending life.

Each of us will one day die, but most of us don't know when or how it will happen—death quickly becomes "out of sight, out of mind." When we're young, we tend to feel particularly invincible. As a result, many people in their twenties live life with only a wandering sense of urgency and an occasional haunting fear of what lies beyond.

It's at this very crucial juncture that legacy—the sum total of who we are and what we leave behind—should become important to us. Rethinking accomplishment and success is vital to our learning to live strategically. Now—when we can still do something about it—is when we should be thinking

---

1. I have a picture taped inside my journal of my ninety-year-old Grandpa Richardson standing and smiling beside his own headstone next to where my grandmother is buried. Grandpa is probably more comfortable with the thought of his own death than any other person I know. For years he used to mow the cemetery—including his own grave site—on a biweekly basis, joking about keeping the weeds down so he would have a better view when he dies. He's a man whom I hope to be like when I'm ninety.

about what our lives will come to mean in our deaths. Death is life's great perspective bringer.

Greatness Is Not the Goal

When we get philosophical about our lives, we may shudder if we consider the lack of historical and global impact we seem to be making. We both thought about this after watching *Braveheart,* the 1995 movie about the poet-warrior William Wallace, who led the Scots against England in the early fourteenth century. Recognized as the inspiration for that bloody but glorious revolution, Wallace changed the course of Scotland's history. Sure, Hollywood is prone to elaboration, but the fact that Wallace's name somehow got attached to such heroism fascinates us.

Something tells us we won't have quite the same influence on our country. After all, we can't all be national heroes. Not only that, but there are no more continents to discover, the recipe for Krispy Kremes has been perfected, and James Taylor has written most of the great songs we wish we had composed. Yet we still long to have some sort of impact. Even when we think about the many things left to discover, we wonder if we'll be the ones who will get to discover them. And then, when we read Jeremiah 45:5,[2] we wonder if we should be wondering about any of this at all. Now what?

I (Craig) grew up sure that I was destined for greatness, mostly because there was nowhere to go but up. I was born the oldest of three to parents who still live a nice life on a six-hundred-acre farm and spend their time farming (Dad) and teaching high-school English (Mom).[3] We had two dogs and a cat, went to church with the rest of the Methodists in town, and never paid too much attention to what went on in other places of the world like New York or London. A good life, sure, but pretty run of the mill.

I played two sports in high school with some degree of fundamental competence, sang in the school chorus and competed at all the music contests,

---

2. "Should you then seek great things for yourself? Seek them not."

3. Mom and Dad are still happily married after almost forty years together; this fact may actually represent the only nonaverage statistic of my entire existence.

played trombone in the band, and participated in speech competitions. I was involved at church, worked on the farm, wrote and performed in musicals, and was elected class president three out of four years. I was known throughout school as the talented kid who would one day probably become president or at least make it out of the county.[4]

In my senior year of high school, I squeaked out an ACT score good enough to get accepted to Mizzou, where I graduated with a degree in geography. (I couldn't get into journalism because, while I wasn't a bad student, I wasn't at the top of the heap either.) Regardless of where I was, it seemed that in everything I did, the theme of being average remained the same—I was as common as a cold. After graduation I became a "camp guy" at Eagle Lake, which was a great job, but it didn't exactly come with a good deal of respect from others.[5] As a result, I found myself wondering if who I was, was as good as I got, which wasn't all that bad, but it wasn't exactly stand-the-world-on-its-ear amazing, either. A dichotomy grew within me—a desire, on the one hand, for contentment and simplicity, and on the other, a longing for greatness and influence.

This turmoil all culminated when I turned thirty and had a slight midlife crisis ten years too early. What legacy was I leaving? How many millions (thousands? hundreds? dozens?) of people were living their lives differently because of the way I'd lived mine so far? What exactly was God asking me to do, and why wasn't he speaking in a louder voice? I had made good progress answering the who-am-I question, but now I wondered, *Who cares?* I moped around and whined about every opportunity I didn't have. I submitted an article to *Newsweek's* "My Turn" column titled "The Raw of Averages: How My Mediocrity Rubs Me the Wrong Way." I got so mad at the world one day that

---

4. I love John Mellencamp's take on this in his song, "Pink Houses": "Well, he told me when I was younger—said, 'Boy, you're gonna be President,' but just like everything else, those old crazy dreams just kind of came and went."

5. If I had a dime for every time someone said, "Gee, it must be nice to work only three months out of the year, playing with kids," I wouldn't have had to raise the financial support to do it.

Megan packed up the girls and went to the McQueeneys' house until I cooled off later that night. Needless to say, thirty was a rough year.

Finally, eleven months later, on New Year's Eve, I resolved to let go of my preoccupation with the legacy I *thought* I should leave and instead tried to focus on living a life that a good legacy would simply *follow*. While I still have my compulsive moments, this small but significant shift has helped me relax a bit in thinking about who I am and what I will leave behind. And I still believe that thinking about (but not dwelling on) what our legacy will be provides perspective that keeps us looking up and ahead toward the future.

Now I (Doug) have to interject. Craig and I look at things a bit differently on this score, and to be honest, it has caused a bit of tension in our relationship. I think Craig gets too hot and bothered about what impact he's having, especially when he's always assessing himself against his *ideal* self and, as a result, never seems to be able to have the impact he desires.

His beef with me? He sometimes thinks I don't care *enough* about impact, perhaps because I'm far more tied up in remembering whom I'm having lunch with tomorrow, what committee meeting I just missed, or how I can score tickets for the big game. It's not that I'm shallow; it's just that I don't think about all the things I'm *not* doing or *haven't* done as much as Craig tends to.

Actually I do care—some. I used to think I would either be (1) a Pulitzer Prize–winning journalist or (2) the world's greatest Christian.[6] Eventually I figured out that greatness wasn't the goal. The goal was the pursuit of Christ and glorifying God wherever he put me. So my wrongheaded "dreams" have been dropped. Now my dreams are more realistic and, I believe, more in line with what God wants.

I'd like to think I'm progressing in answering the who-am-I question, that I've finally figured out aspects of my calling, that I'm plugging away with loving my family and church—and therefore my legacy will take care of itself. I see glimpses of a changed life, of God's continued grace to me and my family, and of his using me in the lives of others. That makes me happy enough to

---

6. I also wanted to play baseball for the St. Louis Cardinals, but the travel is a killer.

evaluate my progress and not get too worried just yet. I'm not saying I'm coasting, but the picture of who I am and what I will leave behind is becoming clearer, and I'm thankful for that.

Regardless of which of our perspectives you gravitate toward, the most important aspect of legacy we need to grasp is that we're leaving one already, whether or not we want to. Do we realize this? Do we care enough about it? We should, not just for our sakes, but for the sakes of those around us.

In my ministry I often tell students to sign up for conferences and Bible studies not always for themselves but because other people will go if they go. Summer conferences may be great for them personally, but they also need to see the lights turn on for the person sitting next to them, the person who wouldn't have gone alone. Our decisions can touch and change other people. That is legacy.

We need to keep in mind that it's God's responsibility to determine what our legacy will be; it's our responsibility to join him in making it happen. We should evaluate our lives and choices, our impact on others, and our spheres of influence now and then. But when we've done that, we need to temper the pressure of those opportunities with prayer, committing them to God to do with as he wishes. That might be the time to put those thoughts of the future away for a while if they distract us from living faithfully in the present.

Some people will never realize their legacy. You often hear someone say that the words of another person changed a life, but the speaker never knew about it.[7] Some people will toil in obscurity, and their legacy will be that of faithfulness in the little things. And that's fine. We can't necessarily control the circumstances the Lord will put us in (for example, Joseph sold into slavery, Darnly's husband in a coma, Trevor losing his business, Johnny Savage quitting the day of the show and director Corky St. Clair having to fill in).[8] Circumstances can change the legacy we leave, but they don't eliminate the fact that we're leaving one.

---

7. Marlo Thomas's book, *The Right Words at the Right Time* (New York: Atria, 2002), is about this.
8. See the film *Waiting for Guffman* (1996).

The Passion of Passing Life On

Having let you in on a bit of our quarreling and at least settling on the fact that we *are* going to leave a legacy, let's ask the key question: What kind of legacy do we *want* to leave?

Jesus is the ultimate example of living fully in the moment and also being fully aware of his legacy. Discussing Jesus' view of temporal things can be a bit tricky (being fully God and fully man makes it hard for us to relate), but we do see him continually talking about what things would be like when he left. He wanted the disciples to know that, yes, he would be crucified and would rise again and that his church would continue without his bodily presence. The apostles he'd chosen would carry on his work and mission, empowered by the Holy Spirit.

We get a brief look into Jesus' thoughts about his legacy in his prayer in John 17. Immediately after this prayer, Jesus would be betrayed by Judas, arrested, and begin the final journey to his painful and shameful death on the cross. Yet he stood on the brink of all that and prayed. He prayed for himself, committing his life and death into his Father's hands. He prayed for his disciples, that the Father would protect them as they carry on the work of the gospel. He prayed for all believers of all time, that we would understand our connection with him so profoundly that we would continue to glorify him in all we say and do. Jesus' entire life built toward the legacy he was going to leave. But we're not Jesus.

So how do we give thought to what our own legacy might be? I (Craig) went to my Grandmother Richardson's funeral several years ago, and for the first time in my short funeral-attending history, I took note of who was there and why. The first of my four grandparents to pass away, my Grandmother Richardson had a brain aneurysm that suddenly brought an end to her very healthy eighty-year life. She was a small, quiet woman, married to my grandfather for more than sixty years, a mother of five, an unbelievable cook, an even more amazing quilter, and a strong follower of Jesus. She studied for and received her GED when she was sixty, but she knew what she believed about almost everything, and when she revealed those beliefs, she was usually right on. We loved her.

So did twelve hundred other people, or at least that's how many came to her funeral. And they were happy to be there. Why so many so happy? Because even though Grandma was average or even below average in the world's eyes in education and power, she fulfilled her calling and left behind a legacy of having loved people in a way that only she could. Sure, these folks were sad Grandma was gone, but it seemed to them a privilege to come celebrate her life and the way she had lived it so well—with admirable character, a healthy worldview, and all for the glory of God. We could all hope to be so "average" in our impact upon others.

Just as the deaths of those we love can help us think about our lives, new life can help us as well. The births of our children gave me (Doug) a new perspective on this whole idea of legacy. Of course, I want my kids to be perfectly adjusted, smart, compassionate, loving, talented, athletic people who never have problems and think I'm the greatest. The trouble with this is it's not reality. I used to have this view of what being a dad and husband meant, and I chased it with full steam. But then I realized that I *will* let my kids down. I could play baseball with Cal for ten hours straight, and he would be disappointed with me for stopping. The perfect dad does not exist.

In light of this realization, what do I *really* want for my kids? A healthy relationship. To enjoy them and laugh and cry with them. To be real and genuine. To help them grow by giving them tools for life. To protect them at times. To reveal life—and hurt—in its own time too. To forgive my kids when they do stupid things and receive forgiveness from them when *I* do stupid things. To see them marry the Right Person. To see them learn about and love Jesus. Micromanaging all of those things is tempting, but I'm trying to resist, because that's not the legacy I want to leave. They won't remember that I was perfect, but I do want them to remember that I loved them and I loved their mom.

As we consider this idea of legacy, we might need to consider what effect our deaths may have on others. Or do some investigating into who others think we are and what legacy they would say we're leaving. Or consider now what changes need to be made to leave a better legacy.

Ephesians 2:10 says, "For we are God's workmanship, created in Christ Jesus to do good works, which God prepared in advance for us to do." Thus, we colabor with God, but we aren't exactly equal partners in the deal. He may make us "great" or not; regardless, we are to walk in his will and take whatever goodness he gives us, trusting and obeying him all the way. That is a great legacy to leave.

Real Credentials

Paul wrote in 2 Corinthians 3:1-3,

> Are we beginning to commend ourselves again? Or do we need, like some people, letters of recommendation to you or from you? You yourselves are our letter, written on our hearts, known and read by everybody. You show that you are a letter from Christ, the result of our ministry, written not with ink but with the Spirit of the living God, not on tablets of stone but on tablets of human hearts.

Throughout his ministry Paul felt some of the pressure of needing endorsement or accolades in order to be taken seriously in the eyes of others. And yet in this passage, Paul pointed to the people he had helped and declared that *they* were his credentials for his life's work. Paul reminded them of the change the gospel had wrought in their lives—people were his letters of recommendation.

In our twenties we're pursuing external affirmation, polished résumés, and good references. That's not all bad, but the most important thing we can do is build a résumé of people's lives. Degrees can be helpful, but they need to be placed in the context of fulfilling our calling to make disciples and share the gospel. We may need them to do what God wants us to do, but we shouldn't trust in them or dwell on them for our worth or significance. What institutions think of us isn't nearly as important as what Jesus thinks of us. The character and competence to do what he calls us to do comes from God and God alone (see 2 Corinthians 3:5-6).

A couple of years ago, I (Craig) went through several frustrating experiences of speaking to youth and collegiate ministry leaders only to see their respect for me dwindle before my eyes during our conversations afterward when they discovered that I didn't have formal seminary training. Just twenty minutes before, they had taken me seriously because of my sound points and personal experiences, but I became just another guy who was "below" them when they learned I didn't have what they did: a formal degree in what they were doing.

Added to my aggravation was the fact that several of my friends (Doug being one of them) had recently graduated with seminary degrees. I came to the conclusion that if I wanted to be taken seriously, I needed to get credentialed. Having made up my mind to never be looked down upon again by anyone with a graduate or postgraduate degree, I secured my transcripts from Mizzou, filled out an application for one of the local seminary extensions here in Colorado Springs, and made plans to get a new diploma to hang above my desk.

Just before I wrote out the check for the application-processing fee and dropped the envelope in the mail, the Holy Spirit brought to mind several questions about why I was doing what I was doing. As I thought about these questions, I could no longer hide the fact that my goal was not to learn more of the Scriptures but to simply have a title in front of my name and the right initials behind it so I could go toe to toe with anyone else who cared about how we came across to each other. A bit ashamed by my impure motives, I asked God for forgiveness, ripped up the application and the envelope, and threw it all in the trash. While I still hope to one day get that degree, if I do, it will be for better reasons than I had the first time around.

If we end up with credentials or letters behind our names, so be it; they may come in handy one day and represent experiences and changes in our lives that have made us who we are today.[9] But if we seek those things for their own merit as a badge or an idol or solely to be validated in the eyes of others, then we've forgotten our true calling and identity as children of God, which is as important a legacy as we could ever leave for those coming behind us.

---

9. We'd like to point out Paul's *lack* of hesitation to insist on his credentials in the book of Galatians, validating himself by his call and credentials, not just by the fruit of his ministry. An interesting balance to 2 Corinthians.

Dealing with Disappointment

In his book *What Are People For?* Wendell Berry tells of his experience buying some land and looking at it with all the wonderful things he had in mind to fix and change it. Now, years later, when he reevaluates it, he still sees problems that need fixing. But many of the problems are ones he created. He had tried to make a small pond on a section of his land according to the vision he had in his head, but his best efforts made it worse. The pond leaked, the ground slipped. He writes, "The trouble was the familiar one: too much power, too little knowledge." And though the modest damage will heal, he grieved that he had to undo his own doing.[10]

When many of us stand at the cusp of turning twenty years old, we look over the next few decades of our lives and see our work as fixing the problems we're sure we'll find. We have visions of what our lives will be like and make plans for how to make them work out that way. Later in our twenties, however, we see reality more clearly. We see that many of the problems in our lives are from our own making. We can't blame our parents, our towns, our schools, or our situations any longer.

Added to our missteps are the timing, circumstances, and realizations that make up life. And as we grow older, the brightness of some of our personal dreams—publishing a book, living as a missionary for ten years in Uganda, opening up our own coffee shop—may begin to fade because we are starting to put others before ourselves more than we did in the past. While it's a good thing—even a great thing!—to put the interests of others before our own, that doesn't mean it's easy.

Brian Rutland, a pastor and good friend in Denver, and I (Craig) check in often with each other concerning this area of "others before ourselves." We confess to each other that we at times feel overwhelmed by our responsibilities—living with and loving our wives; providing for, training, and making time for our children; ministering to people and trying to walk with God—

---

10. Wendell Berry, "Damage," in *What Are People For?* (New York: North Point Press, 1990), 5.

and yet we have no intention of breaking free from them. We just desire to accept and handle those callings with more grace and success than we often do, embracing God's sovereignty in our lives and letting go of other options or opportunities (all good in and of themselves) that we may have had once, but which ended up not being ours after all. Ten years ago our lives were very different, but that was then; this is now. Things have changed, and we have to learn how to change as well.[11]

While we may wonder if we'll ever get the chance later to catch up—to *really* impact the world on a timetable and in a way more in line with our initial dreams—we need to be careful not to miss the fact that how we handle ourselves in the midst of change and redirection can also be a significant part of the legacy we leave.

Think of the stories in Genesis 29–30. Leah probably thought her husband would love her once he married her, but Jacob almost screamed in horror to find her in his bed. Rachel must have thought she would continue to be the superstar, but she could not have the children she so desired. Jacob wanted to marry the girl he loved, but he lost his dignity. None of this was what Leah, Rachel, and Jacob hoped for, longed for, or dreamed about. Circumstances, others' decisions, and their own choices all had a part in those disappointments.

And God was at work. Rachel bore Joseph, the one who saved his people from the famine. And unloved Leah, the girl nobody wanted, bore Reuben, Simeon, Levi, and Judah—the last of which was the line from which Jesus came.

If you're struggling through disappointments in your life right now, keep in mind that God might be breaking you of your lofty visions of grandeur so that you will rely on him alone. You're not behind. You don't have to catch up or get ahead. You need to be faithful right now. Your faithfulness today in the midst of your disappointment will leave its own legacy.

A friend of ours, Empress, recently sorted out a bit of her own legacy. By the age of seventeen, Empress thought she had everything figured out: She

---

11. Brian once observed that it used to take so much to make him happy. Now a nap or just an hour to himself late at night makes him almost euphoric. If and when you have kids, you'll understand.

would go to a two-year college, get her paralegal degree, and then go to law school. After graduation she would become this outstanding female African American attorney and then marry someone who was on the same track she was.

After high school Empress immediately moved away from home into an apartment, got a decent job, and entered college, but she didn't know anything about finances, credit, or budgeting, and she began to spiral into a pool of debt. Life was opaque. She had no clear direction for how to get to the future she had envisioned. Instead, she just moved here and there and prayed that everything would fall into place. Little did she know she was going in circles for a reason.

As she reflects on her past, Empress realizes that she had based every decision and action on what she thought people wanted her to do, think, feel, and accomplish. She knew how to boost the self-esteem and spirits of others, but she couldn't get around to improving her own.

In the process of this emotional schizophrenia, several women had come to her with their own pains and hurts and disappointments; they called her and asked her for prayer and advice, seeking counsel from her. All this made her realize that if she was truly going to help someone, she must get help herself. She began talking to others, telling her story, and wrestling honestly with the gospel in her own life.

As it turned out for Empress, being a twentysomething who hadn't accomplished all she thought she should by this time in her life was not all that bad. In fact, she's glad she didn't go to law school and become an attorney. Had it not been for all of her own hurts, she probably wouldn't have realized her passion for helping women in need. Since this experience, she has let go of the legacy she had sought to leave and accepted a new one that God continues to unfold.

Like Brian, like Empress, like us, in your twenties you may deal with a different reality from what you thought life might be like, and that may even include some letting go. Yet there is hope because God can take some of the very things that we would change about our lives and use them to minister to others. Some of our hurts may become the tools we'll need to straighten out our thoughts and desires and get us headed on the right path, perhaps helping others do the same along the way.

The Three GCs

When we find ourselves wondering about our worth and our value, we need to go back to some of the principles we've already discussed in this book. Although the world may disparage us, we can be confident that God is at work in our lives. We must get our eyes off what we have or haven't done and onto the Father—the One who has done it all, the One who has set before us what we will do in the full scope of our human existence.

If we remember our true calling and our true identity, we can begin to see more of our legacy, though it may remain veiled to us for quite some time. We are valuable in God's eyes; we're his own children, precious beyond measure. We have a calling, and as we fulfill it, we are blessed regardless of how much we are paid or what title we wear.

Our ultimate legacy as believers is to be faithful to what we know and to invest in the people around us. It doesn't get much more foundational than Jesus' *Great Commandment:* " 'Love the Lord your God with all your heart and with all your soul and with all your mind.' This is the first and greatest commandment. And the second is like it: 'Love your neighbor as yourself' " (Matthew 22:37-39).

How do we do this? Jesus tells us in the *Great Commission:* "Therefore go and make disciples of all nations, baptizing them in the name of the Father and of the Son and of the Holy Spirit, and teaching them to obey everything I have commanded you. And surely I am with you always, to the very end of the age" (Matthew 28:19-20).

In what context do we fulfill these two things? Within the church—the body of Christ—which Jesus talks about in the *Great Constitution:* "And I tell you that you are Peter, and on this rock I will build my church, and the gates of Hades will not overcome it" (Matthew 16:18).

Putting these three GCs together to form our legacy means that, as we grow in our understanding of who we are and who God is, we pursue love of

God and love of people. We share the good news of Christ with those who don't know him. We teach and disciple those who come to faith in him. All this happens as the church moves forward into the world.

Our legacy? Sure, some of us will paint masterpieces or establish championship football teams. Others will fulfill callings as mothers, lawyers, ski instructors, janitors, nutritionists. Some of those roles will be considered great by the world's standards and others perhaps not. What matters is who we will become and how we will influence others in the process of fulfilling our primary calling, "to glorify God and enjoy Him forever,"[12] for this is the only lasting legacy we can hope to leave.

Ideas of Things to Do

- Begin with the end in mind. Try writing a draft of your obituary. What would you like others to say about you when you're gone?
- If you have kids, be intentional about raising them. Don't abdicate their development to others.
- Set goals for yourself and check periodically to see if you're accomplishing them.
- Read books about great people from the past. There's a reason you've heard of them!
- Spend time with kids, regardless of their ages. There is no more needy audience for heroes in today's world.
- Don't be lazy. Life's too short!
- Keep a book of quotes that are meaningful to you in your quest for success. They make for good reading when you're feeling down.
- Pick two or three people each year and make a special effort to invest yourself in their lives. Spend time with them.

---

12. Found in the Westminster Shorter Catechism, this is the answer to the question, What is the chief end of man?

The Thirties

A Look Ahead

I was thirty. Before me stretched the portentous,
menacing road of a new decade.
—Nick in F. Scott Fitzgerald's *The Great Gatsby*

I will act as if what I do makes a difference.
—William James, American psychologist and philosopher

Although we personally have finished our twenties, we're novices when it comes to the decade of our thirties. One of our friends who recently turned thirty says she knew that she was really an adult when she learned how to make gravy. Author Mike Gayle has one of his characters musing over the monumental decision of buying a wine rack when he turned thirty.[1] While gravy or wine storage may not be the yardsticks by which to measure, we have a few ideas about what lies ahead for us and perhaps for you as well.

All that stuff about figuring out who you are and who God is and why he made you, well, that should be coming together by the time you get to your thirties. No more fooling around about that; it's time to get serious and go for it.[2] If you're a bit late picking up this book, no problem; it's good to get started early, but one advantage of doing all this later in your twenties (or thirties or

---

1. Mike Gayle, *Turning Thirty* (London: Hodder and Stoughton, 2000).
2. Okay, we'll give you grace to extend your twenties to include, say, thirty-two, thirty-three, or so, but then that's it—no more, or else you have to turn in your twenties badge immediately and become fourteen again, a fate we wouldn't wish on our worst enemies.

forties for that matter) is that you have a whole lot more data and experiences at your disposal.

With the who-am-I question more clearly answered, it's time to take information we've gathered and begin to apply it. We should find ourselves moving toward answering the question, Where is my place? This is probably the question you've been wondering about in the back of your head (not to mention been peppered with since high school), so go for it. We never really put the who-am-I question to bed since we should always seek to discover new things about ourselves, but the Where-is-my-place? question can receive more of our gusto now.[3]

Not Forgetting from Whence We Came

We need to keep in mind the characteristics and qualities we sought to develop in our twenties as we seek to find our place in our thirties. Chances are, as we move out of our twenties into our thirties, we'll start to make more money, but what sense of mission do we have for that treasure? How will we treat our coworkers or employers or employees? What sense will we have of taking care of the earth or our place in the church or community? How will we treat our families and our relationships? Now that life is more complicated, how can we juggle our priorities and make progress in doing all the things we've talked about in this book? Here's our advice:

God first. Jesus as Lord. Holy Spirit as Friend. Nothing—no opportunity, no failure—can or should take the place that belongs to our first love. Obedience is important; grace even more so. Humility, integrity, teachability, faithfulness. Noses in the Word, times in prayer—these have been important to us in the past and should be into the future as well. Church matters, as it's an expression of our connection to the body of Christ and a place for us to find community in giving and receiving. Life is to be lived in the context of eternity and our relationship with Jesus.

---

3. Thanks to Paul Stanley for identifying the question of our thirties and giving us permission to share it.

Family comes next. We should never sacrifice our families for our careers, but we should be people who would sacrifice careers for our families. When kids come, we need to read to, play with, discipline, and affirm them. We should pray for them that they will come to obey God and us as well as learn to love Jesus every day of their lives, growing in that love more and more each day. We need to treat them as unique, created with special abilities that we can help nurture and develop. We should never take our spouses for granted. This is a busy decade—probably the busiest if we have kids—so we need to be even more intentional and diligent to take short bed-and-breakfast vacations, write love notes like we used to, and give backrubs. We should fight for our marriages and for the intimacy we need to be the team we're meant to be, loving each other better and fuller than we ever have.

Next, we need to make a values list about other stuff: people come before things; experiences come before toys and gadgets. We want to handle our time and our money well, being generous with both. We want to live life to the fullest and always be learning and reading and experiencing new things. We want our children to grow up knowing their grandparents and aunts and uncles if at all possible. We want to smoke a pipe every once in a while, even though we know it might be bad for our health. And while we don't want to obsess over every food detail and become so annoying that people don't want to be around us, at the same time we don't want to get so out of shape and overweight that somebody gives us a Goodyear T-shirt for Christmas.

Other values: We want to do something that matters in the world, leaving behind a few people who will remember us for having made a difference for the better in their lives. We want our jobs to reflect our callings and personalities, and we want to like them so much that they don't even seem like jobs most of the time. We want to care about other people's work and help them find their callings too. We want to do the things that are still undone from our "100 Things to Do in Your Twenties" list, and we want to be able to say, "The thirties have been our favorite decade of all" (until we hit our fifties and reflect back on our forties and so on).

We want to read and write and create. We want to live simply, taking vacations in *other* peoples' lake homes and water-skiing behind *their* boats. We want our kids to grow up loving their mom and dad, knowing they have a place to go to when they're in trouble and a place to celebrate when they succeed. We want to continue to know our parents and our in-laws, spending time with them and enjoying them in new ways. We want to save and give like never before, sharing what we have with others at a moment's notice and holding everything with an open hand for God to add to or take from as he sees fit.

We want to keep in touch with our friends through meaningful and on-going conversation and intentional time together, not just through Christmas cards or annual newsletters. We want to make friends in different parts of the world. We want to know God more, to understand him and his grace in deeper ways, and to have that knowledge permeate our heads, our hearts, and our interactions with people—both friends and strangers. We want to get a fuller grasp of the Bible and be able to communicate its message to others.

We want to be able to answer the who-am-I question on a moment's notice, with insightful and wonderful stories of how we've discovered who God has made us to be. We want him to continue to reach into the crevices of our hearts that we've left untouched and work new things in there, changing us more and more. We want to be able to laugh and cry, hopefully at the appropriate times. We want to see new generations of Christians in all areas of life making an impact for Christ in their communities. We want to see our kids become the people God meant for them to be and our spouses blossom to their fullest. We want to travel and meander through uncharted territory, staying in towns that are not on the map (preferably in the Alps or on the shores of the Mediterranean). We want to be less sarcastic and critical and more affirming and interested in others. And we want to allow ourselves to fail, as much as that stinks. These are just some of our hopes and dreams. What, might we ask, are some of yours?[4]

---

4. Keep in mind that even though some of these values are general, they are the expressions of *our* personal values, which we share with you as a guide; you'll have to come up with your own list.

A Final Thought

Remember graduating from high school? We did the whole cap-and-gown thing as the anticipation of graduating heightened with every walk-through. We camped out in the parking lot on the last day of school, making the pavement a campfire and playground. After the day's ceremony, we had our big party in some semicool location where we danced and played and swam and frolicked, thinking that surely this must be the best day of our lives. The thing is, if that were true, it would be incredibly sad, because life isn't meant to top out at eighteen, nor are we to reach our peak at twenty-five.

Life should keep getting better all the time. For us, now more than a decade past that graduation mountain-top experience, life is far richer and fuller than it ever was. We are wiser, sadder, more joyful, less attractive, more loved, more loving, somewhat less angry, more traveled, less frantic, more well-read, tons more secure, at times less conflicted, better listeners, and who knows what else? Best of all, we're not confined to a room in our parents' house in which our bed took up practically the entire ten-by-ten-foot space.

If life isn't getting better in your twenties, we hope it will as you become more intentional in taking stock of who you are and who God is asking you to be. When we have an eternal perspective, we're able to moor ourselves to a rock that is higher than us, to a plan that is greater than we can know, and to a purpose that brings life into perspective as we bring the whole of who we are under the lordship of Christ and all he is.

Who am I? No more discussion. Go figure it out.

Kids

WE'D LIKE TO THANK THE LITTLE PEOPLE

We each have four kids, and most of them came during our twenties.[1] So we thought an appendix on the topic was in order. We don't propose to know everything (or even 12 percent) of what there is to know about raising kids, but as of this writing, we've got eight reasons (ages nine, seven, five, four, three, two, one, and one four months old) to have formed an opinion or two on parenting, so we thought we'd take a shot at it.

At some point in your life, you no doubt have thought about kids— whether (and with whom) you'd have any, and how many you'd have if you did. I (Craig) remember hesitantly entering into discussions about this with Megan when we were engaged. Then after we were married, we finally settled on starting a family in two years. This, however, meant different things to both of us. For me, two years meant beginning the process in earnest. For Megan, two years meant holding a child in her arms. As it turned out, Maddie was born two years and two weeks after our wedding date. Looking back, I'm glad for the timing. In fact, I'm not sure why we waited as long as we did, especially when I consider all that we've learned about God and ourselves from our children.

The truth is, you're never "ready" to have kids. There's almost no way to prepare for them; their presence means a radical departure from life as you once knew it. I (Doug) can remember forgetting Ruth at home once when Julie and I went out to eat. We returned sheepishly after remembering—ah, yes!—there was someone we were responsible for in the back bedroom. Stuff like this really happens!

---

1. Scientists now know what causes this.

Having kids isn't easy—and we're not just talking about what our wives went through to bring them into the world. In our preoffspring days, Craig and I both thought we would be great dads. Renaissance dads. Perfectly loving and kind. Just the right amount of fatherly prodding and grace, leaving our children with little to complain about. Our ideals were shattered straightaway when the little ones actually arrived. Now we know that God will have to work in their lives *because* of our failures as fathers. While we used to imagine what our kids would be like, now that they're here, we're evaluating who *we* are in light of what these little people living with us are teaching us.

And our kids have taught us so many new things about ourselves that we can hardly catalog them all. Our view of time. Our ideas on money. Our views on fashion, education, competition, morals, the media, the Bible, etc. Facing these decisions in light of having children has helped us see that many parts of the who-am-I question were previously unnoticed in our lives. Over recent years we've heard ourselves asking variations of this question such as, What kind of parent am I? What negative things do I do that I should be on the lookout for while trying to raise my kids? Am I still operating selfishly, trying to prove myself through my children instead of helping them become who God made them to be?

Kids require time, attention, and more energy than we can sometimes muster. We'll never be able to afford having them, but at the same time, we can't afford *not* having them because they are so important to our development as people. Just by their presence—and sometimes by their keen powers of observation—they've called out our less-than-Christlike tendencies and created immediate opportunities for us to make appropriate application.

For example, when our kids started walking and talking, both of us realized that we tended to think of them as projects to make us look good. We constantly became frustrated at their lack of obedience. We demanded perfection from them. As we dealt with this issue in our lives, our kids taught us how to love God's grace more. Answering that who-am-I question was tough—we were (and still can be) irritable, demanding, harsh, and quick to judge. When we saw that we had some wrong conceptions of God's love for us, we saw how those misconceptions were affecting our love for our kids. This was an important realization to make.

Now, as we move through this phase of life, we're trying to be extra-intentional about gathering our family, friends, and church around us. We ask our parents questions we never thought we would and turn to other older parents as well: How did changing one thousand diapers the first six months affect you when you first had kids? What did you learn about yourself when you had your third (or fourth or fifth) child and had to go from man-to-man to zone coverage? What are you still learning from your kids? We're also trying to spend a lot of time with friends in this same stage of life; we've had some great conversations at the Burger King play area as a result. Talking with others helps sharpen our answers to questions about who we are as parents.

We've never experienced greater sorrow, anger, or joy as we have with our children. They tear out our hearts and get under our skin, they show us love and loyalty, they crack us up and make us laugh like no one else can. They lead us through the unbelievable and unexplainable experience of being a parent.

As you think about having kids in your twenties, let us encourage you to make Jesus' words "Let the little children come to me" (Matthew 19:14; Mark 10:14; Luke 18:16) your prayer to God. You will never be the same.

Ideas of Things to Do if You're a Parent

- Ask questions as you prepare for a child to come into your house and in all the years following. People who have gone before you can offer a lot of insight, practical advice, and grace.
- Babies cry. It's okay. Your job isn't to keep them quiet twenty-four hours a day. Figure out the difference between an I-need-you cry and an I-want-attention cry, and let the latter go for a while.
- Use the *lexis telionis* rule ("an eye for an eye and a tooth for a tooth"), which translates into "the punishment fits the crime": Not putting away your clothes means that you don't get to pick out what you're

going to wear. Spilling your milk time and time again means you don't get to use a glass. Not putting away your book bag means you can take a Wal-Mart sack to school instead.

- Fight the temptation to have your kids involved in every activity possible. One or two a week is enough. Don't overschedule your family life. Allow your kids to be kids and play.

- Remember that the goal isn't to have the smartest kids but ones who love Jesus. We should ask ourselves whether the decisions we make for our kids are helping them love God and people more or if we have other motives behind our choices—such as making ourselves look good (Ouch!).

- Read to your kids as much as possible. Help them imagine. Teach them *how* to think as well as *what* to think.

- Try to involve your children in church. Sing the hymns and songs at home so your kids will recognize the music in church and want to sing along.

- Talk to your kids all the time. Work through problems. Hear what they have to say.

- Take your kids on dates individually and make them feel special.

- Try to avoid giving your kids everything they want. They should always feel loved and cared for, but they don't need every toy possible. Cultivate generosity and a perspective that cares for others. Look for ways you can model this yourself.

- Think through the various schooling options and get advice and counsel from all sides. Your kids' educations will be a huge part of their developing worldview, so it's important to figure out what works best for them *and* you.

- Pray, pray, pray.

100 Things to Do
in Your Twenties

You've probably done some of these already; the rest can be something to shoot for. And then, of course, you may want to add another one hundred of your own...

1. See the Grand Canyon.
2. Get the libretto, learn the words, and then take in a great musical or opera.
3. Go to Africa.
4. Read great books. Pick out a list and start working through it. (For example, read all the Pulitzer Prize winners. Then read all the Newbery Award winners.)
5. Meet with God every day.
6. Get out of debt.
7. Learn another language. (How about Icelandic?)
8. Go on a mission trip.
9. Reconcile with your parents and siblings.
10. Buy some original art and hang it up in your home.
11. Listen to classical music.
12. Climb one of the fourteeners in Colorado (or the Alps for that matter). (Note: A fourteener is a mountain that is more than fourteen thousand feet in elevation.)
13. Do something crazy—skydiving, swimming with dolphins, running with the bulls, etc.
14. Invest in understanding yourself by getting some counseling while you're young.

15. Decide to marry only the Right Person in the Right Way at the Right Time. Don't settle for anything else.

16. Occasionally give money away when it doesn't make financial sense.

17. Adopt a team and root for them. (Doug suggests the St. Louis Cardinals; Craig couldn't care less.)

18. Take your kids, nieces, or nephews to a game of the team you've adopted.

19. See the castles and cathedrals in European cities.

20. Read through the Bible several times and get to know what's in it.

21. Make true friends and keep them.

22. Recycle, and start a compost pile.

23. Learn to like Bob Dylan. He's worth it.

24. Paint, draw, write, sculpt, create.

25. Know what you believe and why. Truth matters.

26. Pay off your credit cards every month.

27. Swim in the ocean.

28. Pray at the Wailing Wall in Jerusalem and walk where Jesus walked.

29. Thank your teachers.

30. Put some money in mutual funds.

31. Drink strong black coffee and grind your own beans.

32. Learn to make a dish that becomes your specialty.

33. Write letters like songs and songs like letters.

34. See the Egyptian pyramids.

35. Become a member of a church and get involved there.

36. Encourage your pastor.

37. Visit your grandparents.

38. Mentor someone younger than you.

39. Take five hundred spontaneous road trips that don't have a purpose. Just have fun on the road.

40. Plant some roses or tulips or rhubarb or anything and then learn to take care of them.

41. Memorize Bible verses.

42. Vote.

43. Read *The Hobbit* and the *The Lord of the Rings* trilogy by J. R. R. Tolkien at least twice.
44. Listen to Garrison Keillor.
45. Go to a pro hockey game and sit as close to the rink as possible.
46. Learn to play an instrument, however poorly. Take lessons. It will help your other creative endeavors, and you may just love it.
47. Turn off the television.
48. Go whale watching.
49. Read a newspaper every day.
50. Go to nursing homes and hang out with the elderly every now and then.
51. Keep a journal.
52. Record an album of original music and lyrics and keep it for posterity, even if the quality is poor.
53. Send hand-written thank-you notes.
54. Visit your friends where they live now, and enjoy the time catching up.
55. Learn to take good pictures and throw out the ones that are bad so they don't clutter up your desk.
56. Join a local softball, hockey, basketball, or volleyball league. And play nice.
57. Build your personal library.
58. Give away your stuff. (You really don't need as much as you think you do.)
59. Come up with a realistic and workable filing system so you know where important things are and you can find them when you need them.
60. Disable your call waiting and just talk to whoever you were talking to in the first place.
61. Be mindful of the gas level in your car (and do something about it!) so you don't frustrate your spouse.
62. If you're married, don't wait too long to have kids.
63. Call people older than you "sir" and "ma'am" just to be courteous.
64. Listen to good teaching tapes.

65. Fast once a month.

66. Clean your refrigerator and your bathroom regularly.

67. Volunteer.

68. Know where the best parks and used bookstores are in your town and visit them frequently.

69. Camp out every once in a while, and enjoy sleeping under the stars.

70. Always buy used cars. (Let someone else pay for the depreciation.)

71. Hang up a world map somewhere in your home.

72. Celebrate holidays for the real reasons they were created.

73. At least once a month or so, get up early and make sure you see the sun come up.

74. Keep a "People and Praise" file so that when you get notes of thanks and affirmation, you can keep them for when you're feeling blah.

75. If you're single, invite over your married friends; if you're married, invite over your single friends.

76. Eat popcorn and apples on Sunday nights.

77. Attend community theater, no matter what the review in the local paper says.

78. Call talk-radio shows and make good points if you get on.

79. Allow people at least one quirk.

80. Start a book club with nonbelievers.

81. Be gracious (especially in public) when you don't get your way.

82. Sew together a blanket out of all your old T-shirts so you don't have to throw them away just because you don't wear them anymore.

83. If you have a hobby, invest in good equipment so you can do it well.

84. Throw a surprise party for someone.

85. Try to develop the habit of eating meals at the same times each day (this will help if and when you ever start eating regularly with someone else later on in life).

86. Get a library card and use it at least once a month.

87. Take walks.

88. Get to know the person who delivers your mail.

89. Go to free art shows and pretend you're at the Louvre.

90. Get some of your wedding pictures taken in black and white.
91. When you eat out, forgo the chains and support local establishments.
92. If you own a vehicle, keep it from becoming a pigsty.
93. Go to the dentist and the eye doctor regularly.
94. Bring doughnuts or bagels to the office for your coworkers every now and then.
95. Sing hymns or original songs to your kids before you go to bed.
96. Seek out someone to mentor you.
97. Look at your baby pictures and reflect on where you've been since they were taken.
98. Talk to store clerks.
99. Start to memorize the Westminster Shorter Catechism.
100. In everything you do, seek to answer the question, Who am I?

Good Books to Read
in Your Twenties

Novels (Fiction)

We have one disclaimer: There is cursing, sex, and violence in several of these books. But we think it's important to read them since there is cursing, sex, and violence in the world and in our hearts as well. Be forewarned: Some of these aren't G-rated novels as they have themes and stories you need to think about and wrestle with. We've marked with an asterisk (*) the ones that may contain some offensive material.

All the King's Men, Robert Penn Warren (New York: Harcourt, 2002).
>   A classic political novel.

Brave New World, Aldous Huxley (New York: HarperCollins, 1998).
>   A vision of the future that is frightening…and close.

The Brothers Karamazov, Fyodor Dostoyevsky (New York: Viking, 2003).
>   If you can make it through the first half, it's well worth it.

The Chronicles of Narnia, C. S. Lewis (New York: HarperCollins, 1994).
>   These stories are a must-read at any age.

*The Confessions of Nat Turner, William Styron (New York: Random House, 1994). A slave's escape and rebellion.

Cry, the Beloved Country, Alan Paton (New York: Simon & Schuster, 1995).
>   An African struggle of respect and dignity.

*East of Eden, John Steinbeck (New York: Viking, 2003). Cain and Abel, Abel and Cain, then Cain and Abel again.

The Grapes of Wrath, John Steinbeck (New York: Penguin, 1999). And you think you've got problems.

The Great Gatsby, F. Scott Fitzgerald (New York: Simon & Schuster, 1999). What happens when our twenties go bad.

*The Handyman, Carolyn See (New York: Ballantine, 2000). A story about the shaping of an artist in his twenties by a summer's experiences.

The Hitchhiker's Guide to the Galaxy trilogy, Douglas Adams (New York: Ballantine, 1995). Hilarious space novels.

The Invisible Man, Ralph Ellison (New York: Random House, 1994). When no one sees you because of your skin color.

The Last Gentleman, Walker Percy (New York: St. Martin's Press, 1999). Look for the Christian themes.

Life of Pi, Yann Martel (New York: Harcourt, 2003). A boy and a Bengal tiger share a lifeboat for 227 days—seriously.

*Lonesome Dove, Larry McMurtry (New York: Simon & Schuster, 2000). The earthy West.

The Lord of the Rings trilogy, J. R. R. Tolkien (Boston: Houghton Mifflin, 2002). Great stories and characters by the daddy of fantasy.

*Love Medicine, Louise Erdrich (New York: HarperCollins, 2001). American Indians novel.

My Name Is Asher Lev (New York: Knopf, 2003) and *The Gift of Asher Lev* (New York: Ballantine, 1997), Chaim Potok. Two wonderful books detailing the life, culture, and transition of a Jewish artist from boyhood to adulthood.

O Pioneers! Willa Cather (Boston: Houghton Mifflin, 1997). Nebraska fever, corn, windmills, and life for a pioneer woman.

The Once and Future King, T. H. White (New York: Penguin, 1958). King Arthur, Merlin, Guinevere, this book has them all.

Peace Like a River, Leif Enger (New York: Grove/Atlantic, 2002). A son sees his father's miracles and his brother's flight.

*The Pillars of the Earth, Ken Follett (New York: Penguin Putnam, NAL, 2002. Medieval times and building cathedrals.

The Power of One, Bryce Courtenay (New York: Ballantine, 1996). South
   Africa (also a movie).

Skipping Christmas, John Grisham (New York: Doubleday, 2001). A favorite
   of Craig's; check out the tensions in trying to pull out of the culture of
   Christmas.

So Big, Edna Ferber (New York: HarperCollins, 2000). Life on the plains for
   an adventurous woman brought low by life.

*Song of Solomon, Toni Morrison (New York: Knopf, 1995). Morrison
   captures so much of her black heritage.

*The Source, James Michener (New York: Random House, 2002). Historical
   novel tracing the Israelites.

Suttree, Cormac McCarthy (New York: Random House, 2002). Life's
   million pieces never come together for ol' Suttree.

Tom Jones, Henry Fielding (New York: Random House, 1991). Probably
   the first true novel ever written.

*Trinity, Leon Uris (New York: Bantam Dell, 1983). The pain of Ireland.

*Turning Thirty, Mike Gayle (London: Hodder and Stoughton, 2000). A
   thought-provoking take from England on the big 3-0.

Zen and the Art of Motorcycle Maintenance, Robert Pirsig (New York:
   HarperCollins, 2000). Witty.

Life, Culture, Thinking, Musing

Amusing Ourselves to Death, Neil Postman (New York: Penguin, 1986). A
   fascinating history of communication.

Bird by Bird, Anne Lamott (New York: Random House, 1995). Some
   instructions on writing and life.

The Color of Water, James McBride (New York: Penguin Putnam, 1996).
   Growing up black with a white mother.

Gender, Culture, Ethics, Faith, Frederica Mathewes-Green (Ben Lomond,
   Calif.: Conciliar, 2002). Green's essays develop various themes regarding
   women and gender. Masterful writer.

The Gospel According to the Simpsons, Mark Pinsky (Louisville, Ky.: Westminster John Knox, 2001). Insight into American Christianity through our most loved animated family.

How the Irish Saved Civilization, Thomas Cahill (New York: Knopf, 1996). History the way you want to read it.

I'm a Stranger Here Myself, Bill Bryson (New York: Broadway, 2000). An American returns after twenty years in Britain and responds to our culture.

John Adams, David McCullough (New York: Simon & Schuster, 2001). Grasp what independence required…and cost.

Life After God, Douglas Coupland (New York: Pocket Books, 1995). Coupland's take on spirituality.

*Making a Literary Life, Carolyn See (New York: Ballantine, 2003). A practical and fun look at how to write a book and what to do when it comes out.

Man's Search for Meaning, Viktor Frankl (New York: Pocket Books, 1997). Frankl explores what makes us tick through his experience in World War II concentration camps.

Material World: A Global Family Portrait, Peter Menzel (San Francisco: Sierra Club Books, 1995). A picture book comparing lifestyles of families from thirty different nations.

October, 1964, David Halberstam (New York: Ballantine, 1995). The Cardinals win the Series!! The Cardinals win the Series!!

*On Writing, Stephen King (New York: Scribner, 2000). An interesting nonfiction look at the craft of writing.

Orthodoxy, G. K. Chesterton (Colorado Springs: Shaw Books, 2001). An intriguing and humorous look into life as seen through the eyes of this literary giant of the twentieth century.

Pilgrim at Tinker Creek, Annie Dillard (New York: HarperCollins, 1998). Why am I so shallow? Dillard looks at "how to see."

Raising Cain, Daniel Kindlon and Michael Thompson (New York: Ballantine, 2000). Insight into the lives of boys and men.

Repacking Your Bags, Richard L. Leider and David A. Shapiro (San Francisco: Berrett-Koehler, 2002). Why wait for your midlife crisis to read this book? What do you need to make you happy?

Reviving Ophelia, Mary Pipher (New York: Ballantine, 2002). Insight into the lives of girls and women.

The Tipping Point, Malcolm Gladwell (New York: Little Brown, 2002). How little things make a big difference.

*Traveling Mercies: Some Thoughts on Faith, Anne Lamott (New York: Knopf, 2000). Lamott traces her faith history through its crazy ups and downs.

Travels with Charley, John Steinbeck (New York: Penguin, 2002). You'll see just how good writing can get in this travelogue of Steinbeck's trek across America.

A Tribe Apart, Patricia Hersch (New York: Ballantine, 1999). Stories about the three years she spent in a school system.

Walden, Henry David Thoreau (Boston: Houghton Mifflin, 1960). A treatise on the simple life.

What Are People For? Wendell Berry (New York: North Point, 1990). Berry's down-to-earth thoughts challenge our contemporary age.

Theology, God, Christianity

12 Steps for the Recovering Pharisee (Like Me), John Fischer (Grand Rapids: Bethany, 2000). There is a proud, puffed up, judgmental Pharisee in all of us. Yuck!

The Ascent of a Leader, Bill Thrall, Bruce McNichol, and Ken McElrath (Hoboken, N.J.: John Wiley & Sons, 1999). Character and leadership book, the best we've read.

Back to the Basics, David Hagopian (Phillipsburg, N.J.: Presbyterian and Reformed, 1996). A book with essays on getting back to the ideas and actions that led to the Reformation.

Bondage of the Will, Martin Luther (Grand Rapids: Revell, 1989). Makes you think and makes you laugh.

The Case for Christ (Grand Rapids: Zondervan, 1998) and *The Case for Faith* (Grand Rapids: Zondervan, 2002), Lee Strobel. A deeper look at the deeper issues of our faith.

Chosen by God, R. C. Sproul (Wheaton, Ill.: Tyndale, 1994). Is God in charge of every single thing?

Common Sense Christian Living, Edith Schaeffer (Nashville: Nelson, 1983). Help to assimilate our faith into all areas of our lives.

Concise Theology, J. I. Packer (Wheaton, Ill.: Tyndale, 2001). Filled with short entries on huge topics.

Confessions, Augustine (Nashville: Nelson, 1999). Although he wrote more than sixteen hundred years ago, it seems as if Augustine's living today.

Connecting, Paul Stanley and Robert Clinton (Colorado Springs: NavPress, 1992). Helpful ideas to ensure mentorship in our lives.

Dangerous Wonder, Mike Yaconelli (Colorado Springs: NavPress, 2000). For people looking for the joy and freedom of faith.

Desiring God, John Piper (Sisters, Oreg.: Multnomah, 2003). Can we please God and enjoy him forever?

The Discipline of Grace, Jerry Bridges (Colorado Springs: NavPress, 1994). Discipline and grace? Yes, they do go together.

The Doctrine of God, John Frame (Louisville, Ky.: Presbyterian and Reformed, 2002). Frame looks at God's attributes and why they matter.

Down-to-Earth Discipling, Scott Morton (Colorado Springs: NavPress, 2003). A practical and motivating refresher on how to help people spiritually.

Each for the Other, Bryan Chapell (Grand Rapids: Baker, 2000). A great marriage book.

The Enduring Community, Brian Habig and Les Newsom (Jackson, Miss.: Reformed University Press, 2001). What church should be.

Engaging God's World, Cornelius Plantinga Jr. (Grand Rapids: Eerdmans, 2002). Applies a Christian worldview to education. Creation, Fall, redemption, restoration.

Eve's Revenge, Lilian Calles Barger (Grand Rapids: Baker, Brazos, 2003). Explores the psychosomatic (soul and body) union, especially for women.

Eyes Wide Open, William Romanowski (Grand Rapids: Baker, Brazos, 2001). Engaging our culture, especially through the media.

The Fabric of Faithfulness, Steven Garber (Downers Grove, Ill.: InterVarsity, 1997). How do strong Christians make it? Mentors, community, and a cohesive worldview.

Getting the Message, Daniel Doriani (Louisville, Ky.: Presbyterian and Reformed, 1996). How to study the Bible.

Girl Meets God, Lauren Winner (New York: Random House, 2003). Winner traces her story of faith and its Jewish roots.

The Heart of Evangelism, Jerram Barrs (Wheaton, Ill.: Crossway, 2001). Why do we share? Why *don't* we share?

The Holiness of God, R. C. Sproul (Wheaton, Ill.: Tyndale, 1985). What it means that God is holy.

Hudson Taylor's Spiritual Secret, Howard Taylor (Chicago: Moody, 1989). First missionary to China.

Institutes of the Christian Religion, John Calvin (1536; reprint, Louisville, Ky.: Westminster John Knox, 1960). He wrote this in his twenties in the 1600s (Yikes!).

Intimate Allies, Dan Allender and Tremper Longman (Wheaton, Ill.: Tyndale, 1999). You're married—what happened?

Longing to Know, Esther Meek (Grand Rapids: Baker, Brazos, 2003). Meek's accessible book on epistemology (the study of the origin and nature of human knowledge) helps us know how we know. You know?

Mentoring for Mission, Günter Krallman (Hong Kong: Jensco, 1994). If you can find it, this one's a keeper on discipleship.

Mustard Seed versus McWorld, Tom Sine (Grand Rapids: Baker, 1999). Cultural analysis with ideas about how to live out our faith.

A New Kind of Christian, Brian McLaren (Hoboken, N.J.: John Wiley & Sons, 2001). An interesting narrative on the trappings of evangelicalism.

New Seeds of Contemplation, Thomas Merton (Boston: Shambhala, 2003). Revealing writing on the condition of our hearts.

No Other God, John Frame (Louisville, Ky.: Presbyterian and Reformed, 2001). A discussion about the nature of God, free will, and open theism.

Not the Way It's Supposed to Be, Cornelius Plantinga Jr. (Grand Rapids: Eerdmans, 1996). Superbly written book about sin.

Out of the Saltshaker and into the World, Rebecca Pippert (Downers Grove, Ill.: InterVarsity, 1999). Getting out and sharing your faith.

Powerful Evangelism for the Powerless, Jack Miller (Louisville, Ky.: Presbyterian and Reformed, 1997). Miller gets at the heart of our helplessness.

The Pursuit of God, A. W. Tozer (Camp Hill, Pa.: Christian Publications, 1993). The title is pretty self-explanatory.

Putting Amazing Back in Grace, Michael Horton (Grand Rapids: Baker, 2002). Good and accessible theology.

The Ragamuffin Gospel, Brennan Manning (Sisters, Oreg.: Multnomah, 2000). Do you fully understand the gospel of grace? Take a deeper look.

The Return of the Prodigal Son, Henri Nouwen (New York: Doubleday, 1994). Are you the prodigal or the other lost child?

Rich Mullins: An Arrow Pointing to Heaven, James Bryan Smith (Nashville: Broadman & Holman, 2000). A noncheesy look at a musical genius and a genuine man who illustrates many of the points in our book.

The Road to Reality, K. P. Yohannan (Carrollton, Tex.: gfa books, 1988). A convicting cross-cultural take on the need for simplicity.

The Screwtape Letters (San Francisco: HarperSanFrancisco, 2001), *Mere Christianity* (New York: HarperCollins, 2001), and *The Great Divorce* (San Francisco: HarperSanFrancisco, 2001), C. S. Lewis. Lewis brings the heat.

Scribbling in the Sand, Michael Card (Downers Grove, Ill.: InterVarsity, 2002). A deep book that helps us understand the theology of our art.

A Severe Mercy, Sheldon Vanauken (San Francisco: HarperSanFrancisco, 2003). He had it all, especially love, and it was ripped away. Can God still be good?

The Sovereignty of God, Arthur Pink (Carlisle, Pa.: Banner of Truth, 1976). Pink lays it on the line with gusto.

Spiritual Disciplines of the Christian Life, Donald S. Whitney (Colorado Springs: NavPress, 1992). A helpful book on, uh, the disciplines.

Spiritual Leadership, J. Oswald Sanders (Chicago: Moody, 1999). A great book to help us learn to lead others spiritually.

True Spirituality (and anything else by Schaeffer), Francis Schaeffer (Wheaton, Ill.: Tyndale, 2001). Deep, deep stuff. Real deep!

The Trivialization of God, Donald McCullough (Colorado Springs: Nav-Press, 1995). Wonderfully written book on the dangerous illusion of a manageable deity.

Understanding Today's Youth Culture, Walt Mueller (Wheaton, Ill.: Tyndale, 1999). Making sense of where you got your worldview.

What If Jesus Had Never Been Born? James Kennedy (Nashville: Nelson, 2001). Reasoning to contradictions.

About the Authors

CRAIG DUNHAM attended the University of Missouri in Columbia, where he graduated with a bachelor's degree in geography. It was at Mizzou that Craig met Doug, and both served with The Navigators after graduation.

Craig is currently the director of programs and marketing for the Glen Eyrie Group, the camping/conference ministry of The Navigators. A musician and songwriter, Craig has recorded five original albums and enjoys reading, writing, and teaching. *TwentySomeone* is his first book. Craig and his wife, Megan, have four daughters and live in Colorado Springs.

DOUG SERVEN received a bachelor's degree in journalism from the University of Missouri in Columbia and a master of divinity from Covenant Theological Seminary in St. Louis. He then served as director for Covenant Seminary's Youth in Ministry Institute (YIMI), a program designed to interest high-school students in theology.

Doug currently is the Reformed University Fellowship (RUF) campus minister at the University of Oklahoma and is an ordained minister in the Presbyterian Church in America (PCA). He enjoys all sports and loves to read, drink dark beverages, travel, and discuss life. *TwentySomeone* is his first book. Doug and his wife, Julie, have four children and live in Norman, Oklahoma.

For the latest information on TwentySomeone conferences, seminars, and events, or to contact Craig and Doug, visit www.twentysomeone.com.